Martin Saunders has been a youth specialist and serial youth leaders and young people. He's part of the leadership team of Youthscape, a national charity working for the positive transformation of all young people. His previous books include *Youth Work from Scratch*, *The Beautiful Disciplines* and *500 Prayers for Young People*. Martin is married to Jo and they have four children. They live in Surrey, where Martin is currently Youth Team Leader at St Mary's Church, Reigate.

*

The Man You're Made To Be

spck

Martin Saunders

First published in Great Britain in 2019

Society for Promoting Christian Knowledge
36 Causton Street
London SW1P 4ST
www.spckpublishing.co.uk

British Library Cataloguing-in-Publication Data
A catalogue record for this book is available from the British Library

ISBN 978-0-281-08220-9
eBook ISBN 978-0-281-08221-6

1 3 5 7 9 10 8 6 4 2

Typeset by Manila Typesetting Company
Printed in Great Britain by Jellyfish Print Solutions

eBook by Manila Typesetting Company

Produced on paper from sustainable forests

For Joel, Samuel and Zachary –
our kind, adventurous, wonder-filled sons.

And for Naomi –
our fearless, hilarious, brilliant daughter.

May you all grow up in a world
where men know who they are,
and what they're made for

Contents

Foreword

This is the book I was supposed to write.

Although I write books that are mainly for young women, it's not only girls who struggle to know how to live well when they're continually under pressure to conform and perform. So, the chance to write something that encourages young men to step up and step out into the adventure of leading in their own lives – are you kidding me? I'm all over that!

Except that me writing *The-Book-for-Lads* was never going to happen.

Not because I don't care about guys but mostly because I'm not male. Which matters. Lived experience isn't the only source of wisdom but it's a rich one. Another guy telling you that being you is enough – that you really don't need to be that kind of man – is helpful. Maybe even enlightening. Who knows? Focusing on the wisdom in the pages of a book that covers everything – from 'How to feel more confident in your own (not Batman's) abilities' to 'Why sex (or at least porn's version of sex) seems to be everywhere' and 'What to do about the way some men (not all) abuse their power' – might even change your life.

In fact, I want to go on record to say that this book will change your life . . . if you read it. It's that good. Which is why I'm happy I didn't write this book, because my good friend Martin did. And what he writes comes from a place of experience, study, anger, failure, achievement and a deep obedience to Jesus that costs him. He also doesn't take himself too seriously, even though he takes what he writes seriously.

But I know that there's an expectation in our culture that guys don't need this kind of input. Or don't want it. That, somehow, chatting about real life in a real way is not for real guys (whatever that means!). Don't believe a word of it: we live in a world where *Love Island* makes sense and presidents can joke about groping women and get away with it, so it takes a brave person to dare to think that there's more to being a man than that. And bravery like that needs cheering on and empowering – and this is exactly what Martin does.

My advice, as you start reading this book, is to be up-front with yourself about who it is you want to be. If you can, why not decide to read with the option of believing and then acting on whatever challenges or inspires you? This will make you one of those radical men who – seeing the mould that others would like them to live and die in – shrugs his shoulders, curious instead about the life God wants to lead him into.

I want every guy to read this book. I want everyone who cares about the young men in their networks to read this book. Imagine a world where a teenage Donald Trump had read this book! How different might the world be right now?

It's a truly excellent book and I do wish I'd written it.

And my prayer is that you discover something about the man you're made to be that will go deep and stay with you for longer than anything offered by the culture around you.

Rachel Gardner
Director of National Work
Youthscape

Read this bit first

Let's be entirely honest; we all skip introductions. I could have almost got away with starting this book with a page of Knock Knock jokes.* But on the outside chance that you might be one of those people who reads the author's note, I'm going to take a moment to talk about the title of this book which, would you believe, works on two completely separate levels. That's right. Two.

*The greatest ever of these is of course still: 'Knock, Knock' / 'Who's there?' / 'I dunnup.' Case closed.

There's one key word in the title, but it isn't 'man' as you might expect, but 'made'. You see, this is a book about the man you're made to be, but it's also about the man you're *made* to be.

Maybe I should try to explain that a little better. Partly, this book is about questioning, and maybe challenging, the version of 'man' that our culture tries to shape us into. The muscular, meat-headed masculinity of the past doesn't seem to fit many of us any more, but in so many ways the world we live in still tries to force us into that costume. So much has changed; we've had our eyes opened to the toxicity of the male-dominated (let's be honest, *white*-male-dominated) world, but at the same time so many of the expectations and attitudes of the old way of doing things still remain.

A 2017 article on the 'clickbait' website Buzzfeed found a whole range of gift products around the Internet aimed specifically at men, which prove that we're not quite as progressive as we might have thought. There were 'earplugs for men', which are identical to normal earplugs, but marketed at guys who use power tools and play shooting sports. There was 'Mancan' – wine in a can, so that men feel permitted to drink a usually female-favoured beverage. And you could even buy a bath bomb made in the shape of a hand grenade because the idea of a bath 'bomb' clearly wasn't militaristic and masculine enough on its own.

That might be funny, but the gentler form of this gender stereotyping is familiar to all of us. From the moment you were handed your first blue baby soother, you've been slowly shaped by a thousand tiny (or not so tiny) moments that subtly reinforced this idea of what a man *should* be. As we've all grown up, there has always been a loud soundtrack playing in the background, telling us who we are and who we'll become, mainly on the basis that we are part of the half of the world that happens to have a penis. Action Man.* Overwhelmingly male-led superhero movies. The sport that fans and TV companies actually seem to care about.

See how I put those three words together? Sadly, that's the closest Action Man will ever come to having a penis.

It might be that you feel pretty comfortable in the blue-for-boys, power tool, shooting and fishing mould of masculinity. It might be that all these stereotypes don't just shape you, but complement you. You might actually be a guy who likes all those things, and that's

OK – it's more than OK actually. But it might also be that you don't identify with any of this stuff. That your favourite smell is fresh cut flowers and your favourite movie genre is the romcom. Or that you love historical fiction. Or sushi. Or lawn bowls. And if you're one of those guys, then you've probably felt at least a little tension in your life between the person you are, and the man you perceive that you're *meant* to be.

The point is that, whoever you are, you're being programmed to be a certain kind of man, and this book is a chance to consider what it might look like to override that programming. It maybe offers you a moment to ask: What kind of man am I being shaped to be? How much say have I really had in that process? And is that *really* who I want to become?

But that's not all it's about. Because while you're moulded inescapably by the culture you're growing up in, that's not actually what makes you. Or at least, that's not who *made* you.

I should probably get this out of the way now because otherwise it's just going to get awkward. I believe that you didn't happen by accident. I believe that you were made. Handmade actually, on purpose, by a Creator.* A God who made you as his child, whom he loves just like a really great father loves his son or daughter. Except much better than that. Think of the best, most loving parent you know (I pray they're your own, but I understand they might not be) and multiply the way they feel about and love their kids by a million. He made you, and he loves you, more than you could ever possibly get your head around.

Oh man. If you're not actually a Christian, and someone has given you this book, then all your hackles are currently up. If this is you, don't worry. I promise not to lay it on too thick, and you can absolutely make it through this book as someone who believes God is as plausible as the existence of unicorns.

He didn't make you randomly either. You were made for a reason. There's a point and a purpose to your life, and like all good parents, he wants to help you discover it. This book is going to look at what that means; we're going to explore the adventure that God calls us to – both guys and girls; men and women – and the passionate desire that he has to see you reach a potential far greater than the tiny, boxed-in version of your future that modern life will offer you.

The other thing to say, right at the start, is that he's not finished making you. Sure, he made you, but he's still going with the creative process. He's like a sculptor who keeps adding more definition and detail to a masterpiece. He's got plans to make you even better, even more brilliant than you already are. All he needs you to do is trust him with the chisel.

So that's what this book is all about. It's about the man you're made to be, but it's also about the man you're *made* to be. It's about stepping back and taking a good look at the world we're all growing up in, and asking whether the claims it makes about being and becoming a man are helpful or harmful. It's about considering who you really are, and what kind of man you want to become. And it's about asking the biggest, most important question of all: Did God make me for more than this?

1.
Embark:
a chapter
about
character

Batman wasn't always Batman.

Before he became the Caped Crusader, Bruce Wayne was a terrified, orphaned child traumatized through witnessing his parents' brutal murder. It's perhaps the most well-known and straightforward of all superhero origin stories: that awful, tragic moment is the catalyst for Bruce's transformation into vigilante crime-fighter. One Gotham City mugger crosses his family's path, and within moments he's been set on a trajectory that ends up placing him in a sleek black suit, searching for redemption through beating up thousands of bad guys.

Almost in an instant he knows what kind of person he's going to be, and he knows what he's going to do with the rest of his life. Two answers to two huge questions, resolved in a pair of gunshots.

There's been a wave of superhero movies which all tread that same familiar pattern; digging into the early lives of the characters that we now recognize, in order to show us where it all came from. Tony Stark's brush with death in a secret enemy lab; Bruce Banner's exposure to Gamma radiation; Peter Parker's toxic spider bite.* It's a formulaic approach to storytelling, but the formula is regularly successful, kick-starting entire franchises as a result. Each time those same two questions are resolved for us: What kind of person will this character become, and what's the purpose of his life from here onwards?

I love superhero movies. The best Marvel film is Captain America: Civil War, *although* Guardians of the Galaxy *comes a close second. Your opinion is also valuable. If you ever want to distract me from something, get me talking about the Marvel Cinematic Universe. Oh wait!*

In the movies, the answers to these two questions are what make origin stories into opening chapters; in our lives, those same questions can define our future.

What kind of person are you going to be? That's your **character**.
What are you going to do with your life? That's your **purpose**.

Really, that's what this book is all about. You're presumably reading it because you have at least a passing interest in the question of what it looks like to grow up well as a man, and these two concepts are key to discovering the answer. Who am I going to be? What am I here for? If you can figure those two things out, then you'll have a pretty good shot at living a fulfilling life. You might not spend it beating up bad guys or saving the earth from an alien invasion, but you might just get to the end of it feeling like you've reached your full potential as a man.

A great philosopher once wrote: 'Who you are as a person, is how you behave when a grown-up isn't looking.' I say a great philosopher – it was actually my ten-year-old daughter. She pinned it to our fridge one day, I presume in an attempt to shame her brothers. I actually don't think I've ever read a better definition of character though, because she's absolutely right. Our character – the boiled-down 'us' which is seen in the way we act and react to things – is usually most clearly displayed when authority figures aren't around to keep us in check. It's one thing to behave in a certain way in front of teachers, parents, the police . . . it's a whole other thing to remain consistent when none of those people are around.

So here's a question: What's your character like? Who are you when a 'grown-up' isn't looking? How do you instinctively behave? Do you tend to be kind or cruel? Selfless or selfish? Honest all the time, or prone to cheats, short-cuts and little white lies?* Are you proud or humble; authentic or hypocritical; responsible or always looking to blame others? I'm not talking now about the person others know – I'm talking about the person you really are, when a grown-up isn't looking. Who are you?

*I don't know if you're a gamer, but I often think that our behaviour in games is an indicator of the way we behave in our 'real' lives. If you're the sort of person who applies a cheat mode, rather than persevering through the hard levels, it means you're more likely to steal from a sweet old grandma in your street. Probably.

Before you get too upset or defensive in trying to answer that, let me offer a bit of hope. Character is not fixed, it's built. You can develop your inner self, and become the person that you want to be; the best version of yourself that you can imagine. Just because you're a lump of coal now, doesn't mean you can't become a diamond later. So the question then is: What kind of person do you want to be?

Think for a moment about the people whom you really admire. They might be people you know personally, or they might be well known for some reason. I'm not talking about your favourite sports person here, or the musician whose songs you can't stop murdering in front of your bedroom mirror; I mean the people you look up to because of who they are, not just what they do. What is it about them – their personality and character – that commands your admiration?

While you think about that, let me tell you about a couple of the people that come to my mind when I consider that question. The first is my friend Hakan (that's his real name because I'm only going to tell you what a great guy he is, and that probably doesn't require anonymity). I've known him for 25 years – we acted as best man for each other – and I don't think there's any other guy I've known as closely as him. Through our school and university years we were often inseparable and enjoyed various adventures together, and now we're old and boring we still keep in regular touch. I know him really well – to the point that he can't hide his true self from me. The amazing thing is that Hakan's 'true self' is pretty much exactly the same as the version everyone else sees. I've never known him to lie, cheat, steal, or betray or bad-mouth anyone. He's generous, kind, supportive and thoughtful. The person he puts across in public is exactly the same person in private.

This hasn't happened by accident. Hakan is this kind of man because he wanted to be this kind of man. He chose to have integrity, worked to develop his character (he wasn't always quite so well rounded) and he resisted the temptation to take easier paths. Over the years he chose to be kind, to be honest, to be considerate; he decided not to stab others in the back with gossip. After years and years of behaving like that, it just became second nature. Perhaps it's also no coincidence that he's also one of the most successful men I know.

I have another friend who is a Hollywood actor. I can't tell you his name because (a) I don't have his permission to share it, and (b) this way you might imagine that I'm friends with Chris Pratt.* I've observed some pretty admirable traits in him too, and what's amazing is that his character seems to survive even under the pressure of the movie industry's literal spotlight.

*I'm not, but I'd like to be. His speech to the 2018 MTV Movie Awards made me cry. If you're reading this Chris, call me.

He's a great man – a good husband and a kind father – but what's really impressive is how his character intersects with his career. The sort of person that he's chosen to be influences what he chooses to do as an actor; he's turned down countless roles because the scripts demanded that he simulate sex or use gratuitous language. He even turned down a major role in an action film because he realized that it was glorifying gun violence and drug use. This is real character: to put your beliefs ahead of your own financial gain. That movie would have bought him a new house, but he knew that agreeing to it would cost him even more. As a man, he would have been compromised.

In fact, there was even a moment when choosing a shady film role seemed like his only option. As is often the way in Hollywood, the jobs had suddenly dried up for him, and he and his family had so little money that they were relying on handouts from others even to afford food. At that time, he was again offered the sorts of parts he'd usually turn down, and despite the pressures, he held firm to his beliefs. Thankfully, that period of relative poverty was short-lived and he's now got a string of high-profile credits to his name, but his filmography would look even more impressive – in box-office terms – if he'd said yes to every role he was offered.

You might think that there's a degree of foolishness in this, but my friend doesn't see it that way. To him those financial 'losses' are outweighed by the fact that he still looks in the mirror and knows exactly who he is: a man with a strict set of principles that he doesn't break. He knows who he is, and everyone around him knows too. Now every studio in Hollywood knows him not only as a great actor,* but also a great man – and the combination of the two is often what gets him hired these days.

*Stop trying to guess who he is. Also stop wondering if I made this whole story up just so you'd think I had famous friends. Gosh, that would be ironic in a chapter about character . . .

I wonder, when you read those two descriptions, how you feel? Are you inspired? Motivated to be and become that kind of principled, moral man? Or do you find yourself making comparisons; worrying that you could never be as characterful or consistent as them? Do you think: 'I could do that' or, 'I could *never* be like that'? Whatever the answer, my hope is that this book will inspire you to develop your character, and to realize from the outset that building ourselves up like this doesn't happen overnight. Instead, it's about a thousand small decisions, made over a long period of time, where we choose each time to be the best version of ourselves, rather than giving in to the temptation to be less than that. That's all these two men did: one step at a time they acted in ways that were consistent with the men they wanted to be.

So, who are those people for you? Who are the role models, famous or otherwise, who inspire you with the way they live their lives? Maybe it's a parent or family member who has always been consistent. Maybe your family doesn't contain people like that. Maybe it's a teacher, or someone else in your community – a sports coach or youth worker. Perhaps you admire your friends (that's OK you know). Or in the worlds of the arts, celebrity, politics and more, are there men and women whose characters shine through in everything you know about them? Who are the famous people you look up to because of how they appear to live?

People – even these people – are flawed, and it's never a good idea to base our lives on our perception of someone else's. That approach falls down the moment the celebrity we love is involved in a scandal, or when we realize that our favourite teacher has been fired for only *pretending* to mark books for about a year (true story). What *is* helpful is to identify the traits and characteristics of the people whom we look up to, and to aspire to the same. I don't aspire to be Bear Grylls (for a start, I can barely put up a tent), but I do aspire to be a kind, courageous, family man: three strengths I see in Bear which I'd like to grow in myself. I don't want to be Barack Obama, but I do, like him, want to speak up for the most vulnerable. I don't want to be Queen Elizabeth II, but I do want to lead with dignity and wisdom. You get the idea.

So, trying to separate the character traits from the people who display them, what are the values that sum up the kind of person that you want to be?

For example, do you want to try to be more selfish, or selfless; to live for yourself, or live for others? It's a serious question. For some people – like the candidates on the TV show *The Apprentice* – the answer is resounding and maybe even a bit shocking. Here's something an actual human being said, on camera, about their approach to the business-based game show: 'I'm going to throw people under the bus. I'm going to throw people over the bus. I'm going to get on the bus, take the wheel, and get that investment.'

Now of course, we all know that *The Apprentice* candidates are encouraged in those little segments to camera to say the most outrageous things they can think of, but really that statement is just a brutally honest version of how a lot of people actually approach the world. For them, it's all about material success at any cost; they'll know they've made it when their bank balance tells them so, and it doesn't matter whom they have to step on to get there. In order to succeed, they believe they have to embrace a commitment to selfishness, and to ignoring the needs of others.

That's one end of the spectrum. At the other, there are those incredible people who seem to live their lives entirely for the benefit of others. Nurses who come off a 12-hour night-shift and then drop off a donation at the local food bank before returning home to get their children ready for school; charity workers who turn their back on big earning potential to serve those in need for little pay. The thing is, you don't need to go to this extreme in order to try to live less selfishly. It's more about choosing which end of the spectrum you want to lean towards. Selfless, or selfish?

Let's take another contrasting pair of characteristics. Do you want to be known as someone who's honest, or deceitful? Again, that's not as clear-cut as it might seem. In some areas of life, the ability to trick, mislead and deceive others is actually seen as a strength. Take professional poker players for example: deceit is in the job description. But even in business, the ability to get one over on your competitor through trickery is often so valued that those who can do it earn big money for their 'skill'. Salespeople – especially those selling houses – can receive big commission for tricking their customers. If you're practising law, you're often pressured and paid to mislead a court in order that your client wins victory. And let's not even get started on politicians.

Now, although all those industries undoubtedly contain their fair share of liars and cheats, it doesn't follow that you need to practise deceit in order to thrive as a lawyer, salesman, or even a politician. There are wonderful examples of people* who both succeed in each of those professions, and display impressive honesty. You don't have to cheat in order to win. You can decide to be an honest person, and still thrive in a world where many people lie.

I know a businessman with incredible character, who gives far more than half his income away. In fact, he purely stays in the world of high finance because he knows it's the best way he can find to divert huge amounts of money to people who really need it. You don't have to be horrible to get ahead in business.

Selflessness and honesty are noble traits, and of course we should aim towards them, but they're really just indicators of a bigger decision. At the heart of our character, of this question of who we're going to be, is another choice between two poles. Will you be a person of integrity . . . or a hypocrite?

Integrity is simply the idea that we are who we say we are. That we're honest, but more than that, our personality and lifestyle are honest. When we have integrity, we are absolutely consistent with the version of ourselves that we project into the world. Integrity is saying you believe something, and then acting on it; it's practising what you preach.

By contrast, hypocrisy is the habit of saying one thing and doing another. It's encouraging others to give money to charity while your own lack of generosity would make Scrooge blush.* It's talking about kindness but never showing it, or shaming someone else for making a mistake that you've also made (but no one knows).

*If this is not a reference you get, put this book down and watch The Muppet Christmas Carol immediately.

This is about making a deep-down decision that the journey that you're on is for real, and not just for show. Integrity of character is not only deciding that you'll behave in a certain way, but that you'll do so consistently. That you'll be the same person when a grown-up isn't looking, as you will when there are eyes everywhere.

All of this helps you to answer that first question: what kind of person do you want to be? How will you treat others, and to what degree will you put their needs first? How honest will you be? How kind? How humble, positive, calm? And once you've decided all those things, will this be the real you, or just the version you try to project?

What I'm saying is that character is a choice. We all get to decide on the kind of values we want to live by, and more importantly, how hard we're going to try to live by them. We don't develop and become better versions of ourselves by coincidence. It takes deliberate effort and consistency, it takes action rather than just words.

So that's the first part of any good origin story: deciding what kind of hero you're going to be. Once you've got that figured out, it's time to consider your mission. In 'The Summer Day', the US poet Mary Oliver asks us how we intend to make the best use of our 'one wild . . . life'.

Our lives are relatively short, and far more precious than we ever give them credit for. We're born with the potential to be someone extraordinary, and to achieve extraordinary things, if we want to. We get one life, and we can choose either to fritter it away, or to make it count. So what exactly are you going to do with yours?

Perhaps you're one of those people who instantly knows the answer to that question; you've already planned out a path through study and then a career that will take you where you want to go. Or the opposite might be true: you may have no idea what you want to do when it comes to your next set of educational options, let alone your career. This isn't just a question of employment though, of 'what do you want to be when you grow up'. It's much bigger than that. A better way of phrasing the question might be: what would it look like for you to live your life to the absolute fullest?

There's a story in my family that when I was three years old, I would prance around the living room dictating stories to my dad, who would try his best to scribble them down (and presumably make some sort of sense out of my gibberish). When I was eight, I remember being set a piece of homework which involved writing a short story, and filling an entire exercise book with my effort. At 12, I was routinely writing (terrible, awful) short novels and forcing them into the hand of my polite but long-suffering English teacher.* From a very young age, I knew that writing was what I was born to do.

He left teaching shortly after that; I often worry that my Fish Called Percy series of 'comedy' sci-fi novels was what tipped him over the edge.

I know that this realization makes me very fortunate, and places me in the minority. It's important also to point out that writing does not form the entirety of my contribution to this life (and you may already be wondering at this point in the book about whether it makes any contribution at all). But it's the clearest example I know of understanding what fulfilment looks like to me: if I'm going to have a shot at trying to live life to the full, I need to write. Not because writing is key to a fulfilling life, but because *it is for me.*

I have friends who love to use other gifts, talents and abilities, or pursue keen interests and know that if they didn't, they'd be living a diminished version of the life they could potentially lead. They've found that doing these things brings not only happiness, but also a sense of deep contentment. Some of them love to serve others; some love to travel. Some are musical; some are voracious readers. Still more find their sense of doing life well in raising a family, or caring for the environment, or setting up new business ventures, or teaching.

For each of these people, this discovery of what brings them joy is key to their sense of *purpose*. As they go about pursuing these passions, they sense that they're doing the things that they were born to do; perhaps even the things they were made and meant for.

And so we return to Batman. At first, his efforts to learn martial arts, build an impressive arsenal of weapons and vehicles, and network himself into the criminal underworld are all driven by a desire to avenge his parents' death. But as he foils more evil schemes, saves more endangered people and, yes, beats up more bad guys, he discovers that this is his role – his calling even. Being Batman was the thing Bruce Wayne was born to do; and to run away from that would be to deny his purpose in the world.

The same is true for us. There are things that give us a sense of fulfilment, a feeling that we're doing what we were born to do, and we should pursue them. Sometimes they're obvious, and sometimes we have to discover them along the way. You're unlikely to find out you have a passion for travel, for example, without getting on a plane. You probably won't realize that you're an artist unless you experiment with some paints or pencils or clay. Whether you already know what you love to do, or whether you're still on the journey of discovering it, this idea of purpose sits alongside our character at the core of who we are.

So here's a big question: What is it that you were born to do? Or if you don't yet know the answer to that: What are the things that, when you do them, make you feel really, ferociously alive?

It's hard to figure that out sometimes when the world around us is so very noisy. Life is so full of distractions – so many options to occupy and entertain us – that it can be hard even to stop and think about what really matters to us. Do you know what really excites you; brings you joy? Or is even the depth of that question drowned out by a sea of shallow, fun, quick fixes? Let me ask that question a different way: is your life so 'busy' that you never really get a chance to weigh up what matters? In a world where there's always a metaphorical next episode starting in seven secs, do you ever just stop and weigh things up?

I think most of the time we don't. To stay with the streaming analogy, it's so much easier to stick with nine seasons of the same long-running comedy series than to venture into the foreign language section and dig into something completely different, even if the reviews suggest that that dark Scandinavian sci-fi thriller is incredibly rewarding. It's not even that we don't invest ourselves into season one of *Roboternes Udlændinge*;* it's that we don't stop to consider whether actually, subtitled edgy sci-fi is far more our bag than yet another series of *Friends*.

No, it's not a real show. But if it was, I think it would be the story of Dag, an embittered former cop turned private detective who begins to believe that the citizens of Aalborg are being abducted and replaced by cyborgs. I'd watch that, wouldn't you?

Right at the start of this journey then, I want to suggest something. Unplug everything, just for half an hour or so, maybe go outside for a walk, or sit with a scrap of paper, and think about some big questions. We're going to do this at the end of every chapter – pause together and think about some of the questions raised. Given that this is quite a thing to ask of you, I promise that I'll do the same thing. These questions distil the whole chapter down to just a few key points (now that you know this, you can skip ahead and finish the book really quickly), and give you a chance to stop and reflect on all the things we've covered.

I don't know about you, but I find this kind of opportunity to stop and think really helpful *and* really unusual. If I'm honest, I almost never stop completely and think about questions like this, which means the results when I do can feel quite surprising. So maybe you might even want to have a notebook open (because, let's be honest, who actually writes in paperback books?) and write down whatever comes to mind as you try to think about this stuff. Don't see this as a little extra to skip over; see it as a vital part of reading and enjoying this book.

No seriously. Go and do it now. I'll wait for you.

Think about . . .

What is your character like?

What's one thing about your character that you'd really like to change or develop?

What are the things that really matter to you?

What do you love to do? What's the thing you could do for the rest of your life and not get bored by?

And if it's not too huge a question:

What's your purpose? What do you think you are here on planet earth for? What's the thing that only you can do, that no one else can do quite the same as you?

So what did you come up with? Were you instantly able to come up with changes you want to make to your own character, or a strong sense of what you're on this planet to do? Were you able to think of a job you really want to aim for; a change you're desperate to see in the world?

Or did you find that exercise quite difficult; were you left with more questions than answers? Well if so, the good news is that the pressure is off. You don't have to have it all figured out just yet.

Working through the two big questions of character and purpose are perhaps the most profound ideas we can wrestle with as we grow up (oh, and just to be clear, that 'growing up' phase doesn't end at 18; I'm in my early forties now and the wrestling continues). Just by being the sort of person who asks 'What am I?' and 'What am I here to do?', you're already winning, because instead of letting the world around you make those decisions for you by default, you're taking control of your own ship.

When it comes to life, you've really got two choices. Either you let it happen to you, or you make deliberate choices about how you're going to live it. It's a bit like the difference between watching a movie and playing a video game: it's either a show or an adventure. And if you want to embark on the latter instead of sitting passively through the former, then you've got to take some responsibility for your character, and where he's heading.

So . . . are you ready for an adventure?

2.
Who?
A chapter about identity

You are a young man.*

Of course, you might not be – you could be a 'relatively young' man who, like me, still has some growing up to do. Or you might be a woman, who has been intrigued to take a peek at a copy of this to see how men tick, or how the next generation of men are being briefed. But for the purposes of making sense of this, I'm going to talk to you as if you're a young man. I'm also not going to keep doing this – but if you're not a young man, hi! Thanks for reading!

So what on earth does that mean?

Sixty years ago or so, there'd have been a very clear set of assumptions about what that would have meant, and what society was expecting of you. From the moment you'd been wrapped in your blue blanket and introduced to a playroom filled with soldier figures, toy cars and little wooden play tools, your path to manhood would have been clearly marked out for you. Your identity as a male was set and defined.

There would be a set of suggested professions for you, a list of pre-approved hobbies and pastimes. Even the alcoholic drink that you'd be designated to enjoy when you reached 18(ish) was picked out for you. There would be expectations around your favourite sports (or even the idea that you enjoyed sport at all), although there might be some degree of choice there as long as you didn't pick badminton.

And perhaps most crucially, the expectations around your behaviour, and your relationship with the opposite sex, were already set.

Now, there were plenty of guys born 60 years ago who rebelled against some or indeed all of those pre-sets. Men who went into nursing, or primary school teaching, or another traditionally female-dominated profession; guys who discovered how to treat their partners with love and equality; fellas who threw themselves into needlework or netball. But they wouldn't have done so without resistance. They'd have faced mockery – and perhaps worse – for their counter-cultural choices; for not allowing themselves to be bound by gender stereotypes.

For the most part, men followed the path set out for them. Not necessarily because it was easy – imagine being a football-hating, sensitive poet growing up in a family of season-ticket-holding lumberjacks – but because it was recognized as 'true masculinity'. There was a way through growing up, which was recognized as becoming and taking on the identity of a young man.

What's followed over the past 60 years has been a mix of revolution and rebalancing. The boundaries of social expectation were first relaxed and then shifted through the decades that followed the Second World War, and then the digital revolution arrived to change everything. All through that time, questions have rightly been asked of that red-meat-gnawing, emotionally stunted, power-crazed vision of masculinity. So much so, that we all now recognize it as a historical relic; a comic stereotype of a flawed version of manliness.

Say what you like about that old vision of masculinity though; at least it was clear. Growing up, men knew what was expected of them as they journeyed out of boyhood, however misguided or grotesque those expectations might have been.

Now we're not so sure. It's not clear whether we're on a journey towards a new, clear and progressive understanding of what a modern man should look like. Right now the picture is fuzzy and confused. We know so much of the old version is corrupt, but some of it doesn't feel that way, and it's not clear why that is. A more liberated, broad vision of what a man can be seems right, but are there still boundaries to that, and if so, where are they?

On New Year's Day 2019, I visited a particularly tacky giftshop on Brighton beach. My daughter, buoyed by the rare financial boom of the post-Christmas period, wanted to buy some junk for her bedroom which would doubtless get quietly recycled by about March. As we browsed, we found two matching signs designed to be hung in the houses of normal people. The first was a sign for 'Dad's Workshop', where services included 'toy mending' and 'battery replacement'.* It was, of course, resplendently blue. Alongside it was a pink-tinged sign for 'Mum's Kitchen', where a slightly different list of activities included 'cooking', 'cleaning up after everyone' and 'applying hugs and bandages'. This was 2019 . . . and what's more, someone actually bought one of the 'mum' signs while we were browsing for overpriced laminated seashells.

*Incidentally, I have no problem with battery replacement being a part of the male identity. Having enough AA and AAA batteries in the drawer is a proud tradition passed through the ages, and I'm not about to suggest that it stops now. Are you sure you currently have enough? Best pick some up just to be sure.

For me, this was a perfect illustration of why many men experience such a confused sense of identity around what their maleness means. Yes, there are now clear progressive moves in our culture towards gender equality, where classic stereotypes are pulled apart, but there are still plenty of people who think those old stereotypes should be reinforced. So who's right? Are we meant to be chivalrous and practical, or sensitive and empowering? Or strong, resilient and brave? Or stay-at-home husbands who raise kids and write poetry? What does it mean to be a man any more, when there are loud voices in our culture advocating for so many different versions of masculinity?

Well, what if the answer to what it means to be a man wasn't defined by other people, or by the culture around us? What if instead there was a higher authority – one that we could decide to align ourselves to, instead of trying to keep pace with a highly confused world? By which I mean, what if we went back to the blueprints, and asked: what did the Creator mean for men to be like?

I don't know whether you believe God exists, but I'm going to ask something of you from this point on: for the rest of this book, let's just assume he does. It's a bit like the way movies often require one leap of the imagination from us: in order to enjoy the film, you need to accept that James Bond is essentially indestructible, or that one day they'll run Hunger Games, or that Dumbo can fly. At the end of the movie, you no longer have to hold that belief, but the film won't make much sense unless you agree to the premise until then. The same is going to be true here: I passionately believe that there's a God who made us, loves us and has an adventure for us to join in with – but I'm only asking you to make that leap for the next couple of hundred pages.

The reason that's so important is that I believe we can only really make sense of our identity as men if we first make sense of our identity as human beings. That we are created, not just by our parents, but in an even wider and more spectacular sense by the same person who created oceans, mountains and stars. We are not a random assembly of atoms brought into the world simply by biological reproduction; we are incredible works of artistic creativity, hand-assembled by God himself through some deep and incredible mystery. The Bible says

God 'knit[ted] me together in my mother's womb' (Psalm 139.13); yes, science can explain how he does it, but that doesn't make it any less intentional, or indeed magical and miraculous.

Not only did he make us, he also loves us deeply. That can be hard to hear, let alone make sense of, but it's true. When he looks at us, he burns with an affection for us that is basically impossible for us to comprehend. Think of the thing you feel most passionate about – a sports team, a video game, a cause or a YouTuber – or the person for whom you have the strongest possible feelings. Try to imagine and conjure up just how strong your emotional connection to that thing or person is.

Now intensify that feeling by a thousand times, and you're not even close to reaching the levels of love that God feels for you. Again that's quite a strange and perhaps even uncomfortable thing to hear, but no matter how you feel about yourself, or how others treat you, or even what you've done in your life, God loves you with a searing passion. Just so you know, there's no exception to that; nothing you could have done in your life so far that would affect the intensity or magnitude of that love. Even if you've spent the past four years of your life murdering kittens for some sort of sick and twisted fun, it doesn't matter;* God still loves you absolutely.

*I mean, it matters to the kittens. And to animal lovers everywhere. And it's illegal. Do not under any circumstances take the above passage as a justification for kitten homicide. It's not OK.

In the sort of super-cool religious circles in which I move, we call this idea – that our behaviour can't affect how much God loves us – grace. As the writer Philip Yancey put it, 'There's nothing we can do to make God love us more; there's nothing we can do to make God love us less.' Understanding grace is really important to understanding our identity as created humans. We're not only loved until we mess up; we're loved always.

So he made us and he loves us, but there's also something else: he's got plans for us. In the previous chapter we looked at the idea of purpose, that we get to decide what we're going to live for. It would be fair to say that God has strong views on this; as a loving parent who just happens to possess the dual gifts of being able to see and know all things now and in the future,* he has a purpose and a mission for us that's better and more rewarding than any other option. But he's not a monster, and so he doesn't force us into it; it's our choice whether we live for him, or for something else.

*Pretty cool, right? Imagine being both all-seeing AND all-knowing. In superhero terms, you'd be almost unbeatable, or at least, like that guy in X-Men, they'd let you be in charge.

We'll go into more detail later, but in a nutshell, that mission is to help him make the world a better place; a place where good overcomes evil, where justice prevails, where love defeats hate. The Bible says that God is slowly but surely renewing the world to the point where there are no more tears, where suffering ends; where the good guys win. If you want, your overarching purpose could be to play an active part in that grand and glorious restoration job.

God created people male and female – in both cases reflecting something of himself – and while those two are different, there's an awful lot that is true of both sexes. Most fundamentally, it's that we're all handmade and unconditionally loved by the God who is still perfecting the universe, and that we're here to join in with that task. These are perhaps the most primal building blocks of our identity as men, and if we don't understand that foundation, the cracks can spread through everything else that we might layer on top.

In 2014, a US creative agency launched a series of video adverts, which were unified by the tag #LikeAGirl. Partly they were made to build momentum for the women's sanitary brand Always, but more interestingly, they were designed to challenge and show up some of the gender stereotypes that young women often have to battle against, even in these more liberated times. One advert addressed the phrase 'throw like a girl' and showed how both teenage boys and girls still believed that this would describe lame, uncoordinated throwing; but another took a fascinating look at the universally loved language of kids and young people everywhere: the emoji.

The ad showed teen girls realizing that the widely available emoji sets – at least then, in 2016 – were far from gender-neutral. Female emoji figures, the film-makers demonstrated, were generally shown applying beauty treatments, cutting their nails or receiving a head massage. Male emoji, by contrast, were surfing, swimming, cycling or even being police officers. There were, to the girls' dismay, no female equivalents of these.

There are an awful lot of gender differences that are subtly suggested in this kind of way. Superheroes tend on balance to be male, but Wonder Woman and Captain Marvel demonstrate that female characters are just as capable of conquering both evil *and* the box office. Men's cooking and women's driving are often the subject of stock jokes, but leading chefs, cabbies and ambulance drivers of both sexes would suggest that your gender doesn't make a difference to these abilities. There are many things – in fact, overwhelmingly, most expressions of being a person – where in truth, gender is irrelevant.

It doesn't follow, however, that men and women are basically the same; that there are no real or important differences. We are different – in obvious and more subtle ways – and fashionable attempts to totally erode those differences are as much of a problem as out-of-date reinforcements of classic stereotypes.

At this point we need to make a separation, and it's one that has caused great confusion in the modern age. Bear with me; I'll try to make this as painless as possible. Here it is: there's a difference between your *sex* and your *gender*.

Your sex is indisputable; it's the thing that you're born with. You are either a man, or you're a woman (or, in a very small number of cases, you could be intersex, which essentially means you're born with both sets of reproductive organs). This is genetic: the body you're born with, decided within the womb. You can't change this, because it's coded into your DNA.

There are some biological differences between men and women against which it's hard to argue. Men tend* to be taller and broader; men and women usually put on weight in different places. The differing hormones which are dominant in either sex means that body-hair growth is more pronounced in men; for example, on your face and chest. Men are able to attain a higher level of athletic development, which is why, for example, the men's 100m sprint record is always faster than the women's. Those differences are real, scientifically proven and important, and it seems a bit silly to argue with them.

In all of this, of course there are exceptions. I'm talking about averages here. Imagine you line up 100 men and 100 women. These things will, on average, be true. I'm still waiting for the first real flushes of chest hair, after thirty years of post-sport showering with men who have the body of Chewbacca.

Your gender is different. Your gender is the set of behaviours with which you inhabit your body, making you masculine or feminine. And here's where it gets tricky: while some of that is instinctive, and comes wrapped up with your sex, there's very little about either masculinity or femininity that is universal. What I mean is that once you move beyond the physical differences, there's not much which is true of every male, or every female.

Masculinity is much more influenced by culture; by some of those ideas we've already discussed, which have an impact on how our society labels something male or female. Favouring pink or blue, for example, doesn't come from the womb – nor does wanting to play netball or rugby. There's a whole package, established and reinforced over centuries, which is handed to us as tiny babies as a roadmap for growing up as a boy or a girl. But it's created by human beings, not by God or chance. These are not fundamentally the things that make you a man or a woman, although that's the confused idea that we've become comfortable with as a society. Do you see why the distinction is important?

Now, having said that, there are lots of masculine and feminine characteristics that seem to be *generally* true of most men, or most women. Women are usually more maternal – meaning they have the instinct to mother and care for children – and in turn are usually more sensitive to their emotions. Men tend to think about sex more often than women, and seem to be more prone to dysfunctional sexual behaviours. More women than men enjoy romantic comedy movies (although we're all prone to a bit of Hugh Grant), and more men than women have a strange fixation with *Die Hard*.* In all of these cases, it's difficult to unpick exactly how much is cultural, and how much is natural. Do women like romcoms because they're women, or because romcoms are marketed – usually with more than a flash of pink – towards them?

*Rightly, because it's the greatest movie ever made.

And while these things are generally true, they're certainly not true of all men, or all women. There are plenty of men whose greatest

26

instinct is to raise children, and plenty of women who couldn't think of anything worse. Just because you're a man doesn't mean you like football, or spicy food, or cage-fighting, and just because you're a woman it doesn't follow that you're a fashion-obsessed cat-lover with a fondness for Ed Sheeran. The problem is that the world we live in tries to suggest that in fact these things are true – that if you're a real man you love red meat, and if you're a real woman you love shoes. You might, but these are not the things that make you male or female.

At which point you may well be thinking: well, thanks very much. As it is, I'm growing up in a rapidly changing world, experiencing the most confusing and difficult period in a person's life, and now you're telling me I don't even like *Die Hard*. Well, relax: if you do, you do. It's just not the thing that makes you a man.

It's simply that creating a one-size-fits-all male identity has caused a lot of problems. Because as anyone who's ever worn a cricket box* will testify, one-size-fits-all really means one-size-fits-none. And what happens in both cases is an awful lot of discomfort.

It's a plastic penis protector, in case you don't know the sport. Although now you're probably imagining something absolutely horrific.

It's the *Billy Elliot* thing. In case you haven't seen the movie, Billy is a young boy growing up in a poor town in the north of England. His dad is about as clear a picture of the classic male stereotype as you can imagine; he's an emotionally stunted coal miner who sends his son to the boxing gym. But Billy doesn't want to box; he wants to be a ballet dancer – and this conflict of identity creates a crisis for both father and son. For his dad, the decision to embrace a traditionally feminine pastime is a full-on betrayal. For Billy, it means a choice between risking future unhappiness and risking the loss of his father's love and respect.

Thankfully there's a happy ending because Billy (aided by some helpful adults) is able to work out how to integrate his sense of masculinity with his unique personality. Dancing doesn't make Billy less of a man, but embracing his true gifts and pursuing his life's purpose probably makes him more of one.

There's a fashionable phrase at the moment: 'You do you.' Although it can be used to justify a sort of self-centred, anything-goes-if-you-don't-hurt-anyone view of the world, it's a helpful encouragement to move past historic gender expectations.* You are a unique and wonderful human being, created by the God who also designed Niagara Falls and the dragon fruit. You've been given a one-off set of strengths (and weaknesses), physical abilities, interests, passions and your own way of looking at the world. There might be people who are like you, but there will never be anyone else in the world exactly the same as you. So of course you should 'do you'; of course you should be yourself.

Just to be crystal clear, I'm not suggesting that all people who experience a disconnection with the gender of their birth are just struggling with being fenced in by a blue-for-boys world. The weight of scientific evidence would suggest that some people are genuinely born in the 'wrong' body. It's just that for others, confusion around their gender and even sexuality is massively enhanced by the pressures of prescriptive gender expectation. One guy who wanted to be a hairdresser once asked me if he was gay, even though he wasn't attracted to men, because of the stereotypes around male hairdressers.

For all sorts of reasons, we're often made to feel as though we should try to be anyone *other* than our true selves. That our particular version of being human is somehow not quite up to scratch. Ever felt like that? I have. When I was at school, I felt like that all the time.

I remember the first ever Games Afternoon at my secondary school. I was 11 years old, a bit tubby, and not from what one might term a sporting family (unless you count competitive eating as a sport). I was bursting out of my sparkling new white rugby kit slightly, and while I had never played the game, I'd been reliably informed that I would 'love it'. I wasn't sure, but I was trying to be positive, and determined to at least have a go. The games teacher, a tall man with a genuinely and properly cultivated handlebar moustache, told us that before we started, they'd be getting us to run two laps of the entire sports ground (which was about 8 rugby pitches stuck together). The first 20 finishers would be our A rugby squad, and the second 20 would be our B squad. As far as team selection strategies went, it was a bit of a blunt instrument, but given that I'd never really run either, I thought I might as well give it a go and see if I could finish inside the top 40.

I finished 117th. It's a number I don't think I'll ever forget, and the only reason I didn't finish 120th was that three boys in my year were off sick that day. It turns out that I had never developed any physical fitness whatsoever, and this was the moment that I found out.

As a consequence of being slow-clapped back to the finish line by 116 gleeful boys, I never got anywhere near a rugby team, or indeed any kind of cool-kid social circle for the rest of my time at school. Instead I became a bit withdrawn, and a bit nerdy, and mainly tried to carve out a role as second-class clown.* For most of my time at school, I lived with feeling that I didn't amount to much, thinking myself a bit lame and wishing I was someone else. Or at least that I was much more like other boys.

*The role of first-class clown was already taken by Stuart Reynolds, who was fabulously popular for this and a number of reasons. My role was to supply Stuart with the occasional gag or witty nickname for someone else, or to fill in for him on rare occasions of sickness. Socially speaking it was very much the scraps, but it was all I had.

If I could, by some weird feat of sci-fi, go back and talk to my 11-year-old self, I'd tell him not to waste his teenage years pretending to be like other boys. I'd tell him not to be ashamed that he loved computer games – way before gaming was cool, by the way – or reading, or standing in front of his bedroom window with a deodorant can in his hand (oh, don't worry, I'll explain this in a minute). I'd tell him, in fact, to be proud of the things that he was good at – story-writing and joystick waggling and making people laugh. And yes, I might also tell him to go for the occasional run before he got saddled with the nickname 'Fatty Saunders' a year later. Apart from anything else, it would mean he didn't get his own theme song.*

*I shall reveal the words to the song later in the book.

Oh – and I'd tell him to sing. Because as a young teenager, I loved singing and I never developed it. I went along to a performing arts class, and when I realized that every other person attending was a girl, bolted for the door before I ever took a single lesson. I decided that singing and performing was something 'that girls did', and so I restricted my passion to a secret place – the safety of my bedroom.

But oh, the concerts witnessed by that bedroom window, and indeed by anyone who happened to be looking across our back garden during them. My favourite singer – another guilty secret both then and now – was a pony-tailed American crooner named Michael Bolton who was mainly popular with women of a certain age. He was the epitome of uncool, but his songs were soulful and passionate, and I loved them. I would earnestly belt them out over the top of Michael's guiding vocal, imagining a stadium-full of adoring fans on the other side of the glass. In my hand, a can of deodorant – black, metallic, and just about plausible as a substitute microphone – bore the full brunt of my untrained vocals. The bedroom door was always shut; I imagine now my parents thought I was leafing through a secret stash of porn magazines; actually, I was just singing 'Time, Love and Tenderness'.

I tell you this not only to further humiliate myself, but to illustrate what it looks like when you struggle to fully embrace the person you really are deep down: *the man you're made to be.* The real, amazing you gets squashed under a bundle of social expectations, some of which are tied up in outdated stereotyping, and some of which are just guided by ever-changing fashion. You feel embarrassed about what you can't do, and secretive about what you can; you're so caught up in who you're not that you never fully realize who you *are.**

Again, I need to say that for some of you reading this, the stereotypes fit just fine. You like red meat, sport and action movies, and you're aiming for a career in investment banking. If that's really who you are – great. Good for you. Just be sure you're not squashing any secret passions or dreams because they don't fit with the general image of being 'A Real Man'.

I probably couldn't have carved a different path as a Michael Bolton-style soft soul singer. But I definitely shouldn't have suppressed that part of my identity, I shouldn't have felt ashamed of wanting to be different from the other boys in my class, and I should have bravely followed the impulse to sing. Apart from anything else, by now I would almost certainly be making quite good money on the side in a wedding covers band.

You are a young man, exceptions aside. More than that you're a unique person, and even more than that, you're a deeply loved creation; a child of God.

So beyond that, who are you? What is the specific assembly of personality traits, skills, flaws, strengths and passions that make you at least slightly different from every other man who has ever lived? As you answer that question, try to detach some of the 'should's that will be automatically floating around your head; the expectations that other people put on you. Don't think about who other people want you to be, or who culture says you have to be; who are you when all of that is stripped away?

This feels like a good moment to stop and reflect a bit. In this chapter we've looked at the question of what it means to be a man in today's world, but perhaps more importantly, what it looks like to be clear about your identity. So how do you feel about all that? As before, we've got some questions to think through . . .

Think about . . .

What are some of the ways you think you're subtly influenced by gender stereotypes?

In the light of that . . . what do you think makes a man?

How do you feel about the idea that you're created and, beyond that, loved by your Creator?

What are the things that make you uniquely you?

Where have you suppressed or played down those aspects of yourself because of the expectations of others?

Every man questions his identity – asks 'Who am I?' – now and again. That's OK, but what helps us to get through the moments of uncertainty is developing a sense as we're growing up of where we've come from in a cosmic sense, and who therefore we've been created to be. Becoming comfortable about who we are is like putting down a root system; we become strong and developed characters who are honest about our strengths and shortcomings, likes and dislikes. Ultimately you can't put down roots in someone else's idea of what a man should be like, or of what you should be like. Developing your own unique identity is key to thriving as a man.

That doesn't mean, however, that you should just be who you want to be in every aspect of your life. As we discussed in the first chapter, it's not just important who you are, but also what kind of 'you' you're going to be – this is your character, and it's also an important part of your identity as a man. You can be honest about your flaws and weaknesses; it doesn't follow that you have to embrace and submit to them.

At this point, it's helpful to start thinking about a role model. Because not only does God create us and love us, he also gives us an example to follow: his son, who lived and breathed and experienced maleness just as much as we do. That's where we're going next: to the ultimate male (role) model, Jesus.

Before we do, however, it's probably worth saying something about the man that every single one of us must have in our origin stories, although not necessarily in our daily lives. The man who is a bigger part of us, and a bigger influence on us even than we know, but who for some of us brings painful associations and memories: dad.

You can't choose who your father is. Some of us are fortunate to have wonderful, caring dads who play an active and regular part in our lives. Some of us never even speak to our father, and for understandable reasons. Many of us, though, are somewhere in the middle: there are things about our relationship with our dad for which we're grateful, and others that make us grimace. It's different for each of us: every single father–son relationship is unique, and each has its special combination of positives and negatives, highs and lows.

I have a pretty good relationship with my own father, and now my great hope is that I'll be a good dad to my own kids. But whatever yours is like, and however close or distant your connection to him might be, you need to hear this as you think about your identity:

You are not your father.

You do not have to become like him, if that's an idea that terrifies you. It is not a foregone conclusion that you are destined to make the same mistakes he did. If you're the sort of person who enjoys a great relationship with your dad then by all means embrace your similarities and look to him as a great role model. But if the opposite is true, that relationship does not need to define your life, or the way you live it.

If you are a man who doesn't know or have contact with his father, then I'm sorry. I'm also aware that all this talk of God as a father who loves you can feel a bit uncomfortable or even painful. I believe, though, that God's version of fatherhood is so many times better than ours that it is barely recognizable even from the closest and kindest father–son relationship. And whatever yours is like, I promise that the offer to know and root your identity in him is cast-iron. He will never let you down, even if your real father has.

3.
(male) Model: a chapter about Jesus

Jesus was a man, just like you and me.

This is either the most incredible statement when you stop to think about it, or a really boring and obvious fact that you've known since you were 4. The sort of thing that only people like me get excited about while trying to persuade you that it's the most incredible statement you've ever heard.*

I trust that you're encouraged by this level of self-awareness. That said, I do still want to persuade you to my way of thinking: that God is real, and the key to a fulfilling life as a man.

But have you ever really stopped to think about it? Jesus, Son of God – and by some hard-to-understand mystery of the cosmos, also fully God – was completely, utterly, 100 per cent human. An all-powerful God became a not-all-that-powerful human being; an invincible immortal became something that can be squished, exploded, impaled and otherwise ended in a million different ways. The difference between man and God is quite big, and I know which one I'd rather be.

For reasons that we'll get to though, Jesus did indeed decide that instead of clinging on to all that invulnerable power, he'd come to earth as a person. We've all sat through enough school nativities to know that he didn't arrive – like Arnold Schwarzenegger in *The Terminator* – as a naked muscle-bound 30-year-old surrounded by electricity. Although goodness knows, school nativity play attendance would be very different if he had.

No, before he was even a fully grown man, Jesus was a teenager, and before that a child, and before even that a tiny baby.

I don't know that even I – a self-confessed Jesus fanboy – have ever really thought this all the way through. As a baby, he became completely reliant on his parents to keep him fed, clean, even alive. I've got four kids, and I remember just how much poo comes out of them when they're tiny; it's incredible. The only thing they do more than poo is scream the house down; woken by the slightest noise and then up all night with torturous overtiredness. This is how God came to earth: as a screaming little poo machine, completely reliant on his parents for safety and survival.

Then, follow the logic through a little further. Jesus was a child: one of those delightful humans who never run out of ways to ask 'Why?', are fixated with the contents of their noses and underpants, and find the greatest source of possible amusement in their own farts. He played with toys, he ran around his dad's carpentry yard with his arms in a cloak pretending to be a bird (since planes and Superman weren't yet invented). He was an actual, regular child.

That also means he'll have had times when he was up all night vomiting everywhere because he ate something off the floor; he'll have grazed his knees falling off his whatever they had instead of bikes in AD 7, and howled for Mary to come and scoop him up. He probably got a variety of disgusting childhood illnesses; it's likely that at least once he played that really annoying game where you repeat back everything the other person says.

And after that, he became a teenager. We don't know anything about this period in Jesus' life, but we do know that he was fully human, and that his body developed from that of the baby we meet in the nativity story to that of the fully grown man who did all the miracles and came up with all the wise sayings. He must have got there the same way that the rest of us do; through the hormonal wonder of adolescence.

Which means, you've guessed it, he experienced all the same weird growing-up things as you and I. The confusing emergence of hair; the massive mood swings; erupting skin; the frustration of not quite having enough facial hair to grow a beard, but just enough that you look like you're trying. What's more – and I hope I'm not about to commit some great act of heresy here – Jesus probably also experienced random embarrassing erections at the most inappropriate moments. Because that's what 'fully human' means: whatever you experience, he's probably been there too. Jesus wasn't just a man, he grew up as one too.

We don't get huge amounts of detail in the history books – including the Bible – about Jesus' early life. We know he was a fugitive refugee by the age of two, chased into Egypt by a murderous hit squad, and then we get a single brilliant story from his later childhood: we know he went missing for a few days, aged 12.

His parents misplaced him for an entire day – they did the first-century equivalent of driving on from a motorway service station while their son was still where they'd been eating in McDonald's (other fast-food restaurants are available!) – a seemingly awful error of judgement with which any modern parent will completely sympathize.* In fact, Mary and Joseph didn't find him for another 72 hours, at which point they discovered him teaching adults about God in the Temple courts.

*I have almost done this. We were on our way to Wales on holiday, and the car was so jam-packed with stuff that we couldn't see my eldest son in the back of the car anyway. It was only when he tapped on the window, a look of terror on his face and a milkshake in his hand, that we realized we'd miscounted. So, Mary and Joseph, I get you.

A chapter about Jesus

If this were a superhero movie, then this scene would have been the bit before the opening credits where the main character's powers are first glimpsed. In a more Hollywood version, he might have been found levitating a donkey with only the power of his mind, but in truth he was discovered teaching way above his expected level. Mary and Joseph already knew that Jesus was the son of God, but this would have been a startling reminder to them that their first-born child was no ordinary boy. Cue the Marvel intro music.

Between the ages of 12 and 30, we get almost no detail about Jesus in the Bible. All we have is a couple of lines in the Gospel of Luke telling us that he returned to their hometown with them, and that from that point on he was obedient to them; he didn't pull any more stunts like that. All we know is that he 'grew in wisdom and stature, and in favour with God and man' (Luke 2.52). Which means he got taller and smarter, that people liked him and that God was pleased too. Boiled down it sounds like those 18 years were easy; I'm sure they weren't. If I tell you about my teens and twenties in a couple of sentences, I might report the same broad headlines; in fact, the details were a lot grittier. Jesus will have experienced the highs and lows of growing up, but the Bible glosses over that because the details aren't particularly vital to what comes next. What's really important is that when we meet Jesus at about the age of 30, he's a seriously great guy. So much so that he's worth looking up to; imitating even. Jesus is pretty much the ultimate role model.

I don't know whose picture you've got on your (real or metaphorical) bedroom wall, but when I was growing up that honour in my life was taken by Gary Lineker. Now a successful sports presenter, Gary was at the time the main striker for the England football team, and earned a place in my heart for ever by scoring the goals that took the team to within a few kicks of the 1990 World Cup final. I was 12 years old and thanks to his goals, I and my fellow countrymen came close to the ultimate sporting ecstasy. We didn't win of course, but the journey to almost doing so was phenomenal. I can still hear the commentator's roar of 'Lin-e-keeerrrr!' now.

It wasn't just Gary Lineker's goals that elevated him to hero status however; he was also an all-round fantastic fella. On the pitch he was renowned for fair play, rarely in trouble with the referee; off the pitch he was a well-mannered, intelligent family man who seemed to connect with the fans. When I grew up, I aspired to be like him. Perhaps not as a footballer – as already explained, I had about the same amount of sporting ability as a cardboard cut-out of Gary Lineker – but as a man. I aspired to be well liked, honest, a man of personal integrity.

The trouble with human role models, though, is that they let you down. Gary Lineker is mostly a good guy, but I'm sure he'd be the first to admit that he hasn't lived a flawless life. His two marriages broke down for different reasons, and despite a squeaky-clean image, he's made mistakes.* As role models go you could still do a lot worse. But you could also still do a lot better.

*Gary, if you're reading this, I'm not here to judge you. I still think you're amazing and I will never forget the way you almost single-handedly won the World Cup. However, I need to get a life, as you're clearly not reading this.

That's where Jesus comes in. Sure, he's God but he's also demonstrated what it looks like to walk the earth as a man, completely in touch with your identity, character and purpose, and to live up to all three perfectly. He knew who he was, he knew how he was going to behave and he knew what he was here to do. He's not only a God to follow in the religious devotion sense, he's an example to imitate too.

Let me give you some examples; just a few little stories that illustrate not only that Jesus was a good man, or an impressive one, but that he's a guy worth trying to emulate. A couple of tales from the Bible which may or may not already be familiar to you, but that show how Jesus' incredible character lifted him head and shoulders above everyone around him.

For instance, he was very much his own man, refusing to conform to anyone else's version of how to live. Jesus had no interest in cultural boundaries – those walls that people put up to leave others separated and excluded. He treated everyone with kindness and respect, even when it was culturally shocking to do so. There's a story in the Bible about Jesus talking with a woman while she was drawing water from a well. On the face of it that sounds pretty unremarkable, doesn't it? Well, not when you know some of the details. This woman was out drawing water alone, in the middle of the day, which meant she was hiding, or running away from normal social interaction. She was an outcast, for reasons that aren't entirely clear; she didn't want to bump into anyone else for reasons of shame and social stigma. Women would have tutted or laughed if they'd met her; men would have either glared at her or wondered if they might enjoy a little taste of the scandal for themselves. She was living under the oppression of a shameful identity, a local figure of unkind derision who probably saw herself as close to worthless. And by talking to her in a kind and civil manner, Jesus cuts right through all that.

He doesn't excuse her behaviour and allow her to walk away from their conversation. However, the very fact that he's prepared to sit and talk with her invests her with the most precious gift: the return of a shred of dignity to her life. It's a bumpy conversation: she doesn't really want to field his questions and he won't give her a direct answer either. But at the end of their strange encounter* she becomes one of the very first people in the world to find out who Jesus really is, and she runs off into the town to tell everyone about him. That's right: the same town where she's regarded in unkind and unfeeling terms. She doesn't care; she just has to tell someone about him.

You can find this in chapter 4 of the Gospel of John. It includes possibly the most uninspiring verse in the whole Bible, verse 8. I'm not sure why John included it, but perhaps he felt a bit grumpy about being sent on an errand and thought that we would all need to know that for generations afterwards. Go look it up and you'll see what I mean; you won't be pinning that to your bedroom mirror anytime soon.

Imagine living in such a way that your treatment of others actually filled them with life and dignity. Imagine being someone whose behaviour took away the shame of other people. Or imagine you knew someone like that. That's the sort of character you'd want to emulate, right?

Let's look at another, very different example. We see another side of Jesus' character in a short story recounted in both Matthew and Mark's Gospels. You might have heard about it: Jesus finds people using the holy Temple as a place to change money and sell merchandise, and in the words of an east London gangster movie, he kicks off big time. He gets angry, and he gets physical. It's too much to say that he gets violent, but the Bible clearly says in Mark 11.15–18 that he 'drove out' those who were buying and selling there. He doesn't stop there either; he actually flips over the tables – scattering coins and sending doves flying into the Temple courts. Can you imagine the scene? Jesus must have been absolutely phenomenal. We don't hear about anyone stepping in to stop him; in fact, the opposite is true – the story goes that 'the whole crowd was amazed' by his very practical lesson.

Given that he was able to flip huge, heavy wooden tables, Jesus was probably unusually strong – and that's hardly a surprise considering he'd been working in a family of carpenters for the past 15 years or so. That's a little bit of a correction to the sometimes rather puny, meek images of Jesus we see in cinema and other arts,* but it's not the really interesting thing here. What's much more interesting is *why* he chooses to exert himself physically in this scene, and why it doesn't count as an act of sinful anger, spoiling his otherwise spotless record of not doing anything wrong.

A US pastor once famously said that he couldn't worship a God he could beat up, and got excited about Jesus having a muscular frame as a tree-carrying carpenter. This is obviously a bit silly as Jesus was a man of peace who told people to turn the other cheek, and in the one known example absolutely allowed himself to be beaten up. That said, I do wonder if the slightly wimpy version of Jesus portrayed in culture makes us think he was weak, rather than in every sense strong. You could beat him up, but that would just make him stronger. Like Obi-Wan Kenobi.

To understand *that*, you need to know what the guys in the Temple were actually doing, and why it made Jesus so very angry. First of all, there were the money-changers: these guys were running a racket with the corrupt priests at the Temple, requiring everyone to change their regular money into specially sanctioned coins (in order to buy sacrificial doves and lambs). They were taking a cut; the priests were taking a cut; and as a result, good honest people were having to spend extra money just to do their religious duty. They'd found a clever way to add an extra tax on top of the contribution everyone made to the upkeep of the Temple – and it was going directly into their pockets. That made Jesus mad.

Then there were the people selling doves and livestock: these guys were making money out of the rituals of religious sacrifice, and it was another gang-style racket. They would sell you an animal outside the Temple to take in for sacrifice; then when you got there, the priests would tell you it was unacceptable and sell you another animal from their own private stock. So as a worshipper, you got stung twice – and again both the priests and the salesmen were in on the whole thing.

So that's why Jesus shouts, with absolute justification: 'my house will be called a house of prayer . . . But you have made it a "den of robbers"' (Mark 11.17). They've turned God's holy place into a crime scene, where regular people get routinely cheated by a supposedly trustworthy religious elite. He's not happy at all.

Jesus' response here is often described as 'righteous anger'. That just means that while he had an extreme emotional reaction – and one of outrage – it was justified. It was right that he was angry, because his anger was actually wrapped up in concern for others; it was a reflex response to unfairness, injustice, wrong.

It's a pretty explosive thing, Jesus' anger. He doesn't get into an argument, wave his hands around and rally an angry mob. He's fast and he's definitive. He doesn't tell the money-changers to stop; he wrecks their accounting systems. He sees the absolutely corrupt, absolutely immoral way they're acting, and it's as if he has an allergic reaction to it. Imagine being the sort of man who is so morally upright, so sure of your own beliefs, that you literally can't co-exist with this kind of behaviour. You literally can't stand there and just watch it happen.

How many times have you turned the other way when something less than kind or fair is happening? We walk past homeless people without even breaking our conversation or train of thought to treat them with the common humanity of a greeting. We pretend we haven't heard when someone is being made fun of at the next table in KFC, or when something casually racist or sexist takes place nearby. Most of us quietly let stuff slide every day, even when deep down we know it's not right. I know I do.

Jesus just can't do that. He can't stand by and watch the world just get a little bit worse. He doesn't look the other way as someone's light gets a little bit dimmer. He gets angry, he gets involved, and he can't be any other way.

Again, just imagine if you were this sort of person. Imagine what would happen if you didn't just walk on by, if you always stopped to help or to say something when it was needed. Yes, I guess you might get in a few more fights – especially if you started throwing people's tables or money around – but think what might start to be said about you if you concerned yourself with speaking up for those whose voice isn't so loud, and joining in their battles. Imagine how much respect you'd have for someone like that. Wouldn't part of you want to be like them?

One final story, and it's one you probably know quite well. After 33 years on earth, Jesus' radical way of living and talking had got him into so much trouble that eventually it put a target on his back. The people whose lifestyle was being challenged – and ironically, these were the religious people – became so threatened by him, and by the size of his following, that they hatched a plan to have him killed and sent men to capture him. When these men arrived, they found Jesus with some of his closest friends in a garden* in Jerusalem called Gethsemane.

*When I say 'garden', don't imagine the back garden of a terraced house in London. He didn't go off to pray by a water feature at the end of a small piece of grass while the disciples fell asleep next to a rhododendron with Timmy the family cat. Think more of a public park. Or don't; I guess the idea of soldiers arriving in single file through the side gate past the recycling bins is quite fun.

Jesus' friends were loyal – most of them ended up dying for him – so when a crowd of armed men moved to seize him, one of them, Peter, struck back, cutting off a man's ear with his sword.* What happens next is perhaps unexpected though: Jesus immediately heals the man's ear, even as he's being arrested. So here's Jesus, at the moment of maximum stress, being led away to start the process that he knows will end in his painful death. He has just been betrayed by one of his closest friends, Judas, and another has just struck a small blow back. What does he do? Instead of enjoying that tiny morsel of revenge, he realizes that this man is only following orders and corrects his very short-term hearing problem. Now, not only does this action probably save Peter from being skewered, it once again demonstrates Jesus' extraordinary strength of character. Even in the intensity of the moment, Jesus sees the big picture; sees that revenge and violence won't help; sees that there's no point feeling angry at a man who is simply following orders.

This has never really struck me before but obviously this means that Jesus' disciples had swords. We don't know much else about how they dressed, and much has simply been assumed because of what we know about the fashion of the time. But perhaps they actually dressed more like samurai, or like the Mighty Morphin Power Rangers. Imagine that.

Perhaps we might like to think that in a similar situation, after a good meal and a long time of prayer, we too might be equally clear-thinking. But the situation intensifies, and Jesus still keeps his head, even as all around him are probably losing theirs. He's beaten and spat at, whipped and tortured, and then nailed to a wooden cross. And *after* all of that, he turns his face to heaven and prays 'Father, forgive them, for they do not know what they are doing' (Luke 23.34). People are driving large metal nails through the man's wrists, and all he's thinking about is their forgiveness.

If having the presence of mind to heal the guy's ear in the garden was generous, this is borderline craziness. How is it possible to fully experience the agony of crucifixion and yet still have the perspective to love and care about the very men torturing you? Jesus' behaviour in this moment is one of the clearest signs that he must have been more than just a man; no man could show that much character under that much pressure.

Jesus talks a lot about forgiveness; it's a key component of the prayer he taught, and has been spoken around the world daily for 2,000 years since. It's often something he offers to people, through which they find liberation. It's one of the key reasons why he came to earth in the first place. Jesus forgives – and teaches others to do the same – because forgiveness unlocks our most profound and fundamental problems. Forgiveness deals with guilt; forgiveness deals with shame. Forgiveness gives us another shot after messing up, gives us hope when we've lost it, makes us feel clean again after we've done something that caused us to feel grimy. In an eternal sense it's powerful because it opens the door for us to know God,* even though humankind has turned away from him, but in an everyday sense it's also incredibly important. That's why Jesus tells us to forgive one another, and it's why as a man he modelled forgiveness for us to follow.

Yes, this needs a bit more unpacking. I appreciate that if you're reading this as someone who wouldn't call themselves a Christian, this chapter is really starting to stretch the boundaries of our little deal. The trouble is that you can't just think Jesus is a good role model without also agreeing that he was divine, because if he wasn't, then as well as doing all this positive stuff, he went around boasting that he was God, which is not cool if it's not true. So assuming he was God, his death is essentially the thing that opens up the door between you and God. Again, if it's true, that makes him absolutely ace, doesn't it?

Forgiveness can feel incredibly hard and painful at times, especially when we've been badly hurt. I think that's why Jesus demonstrated it at a moment of the most extreme and intense pain. No one can say to Jesus: 'Forgive them – well, that's easy for you to say.' Jesus forgave men who had just jeered while beginning the agonizing process of his murder.

So again, imagine being the sort of man who has such an incredible sense of perspective, he can forgive someone even as he's being wronged by them. Imagine having such presence of mind that you can always see past the short-term pain to the long-term gain; that you could skip ahead and understand the big picture of a situation and how it's going to play out. And if you knew someone like that on earth, you'd certainly look up to them, wouldn't you? You'd probably go out of your way to follow them around.

The point is that there *is* someone like that, and while he doesn't currently walk the earth, he did, and we're fortunate to have a whole bunch of stories about him, and about how he lived as a man. He is, without doubt, the greatest role model you could ever look up to.

This is a really good, practical reason to read the Bible. Sure, if you've ever spent any time around church or Christians in general, they're always telling you to do that. Sometimes it can feel like an empty religious duty, a thing you have to do in order to behave properly as a Christian. But looking at this role-model Jesus, and observing how he lived his life so that we in turn might learn how to live ours, that's actually a pretty good reason for reading it. Not because we should or because we have to, but because by doing so, we learn how to live better.

The even more extraordinary thing about Jesus, though, is that we don't just have to stop at knowing *about* him. That's where it ends with most role models; if you want to be more like Barack Obama, or Hugh Jackman, or whoever it is you happen to look up to, you can watch them, learn from them and imitate them, but that's it. With

Jesus it's different. With Jesus you don't have to stop at knowing *about* him, you can also know him. Because – and I promise I'm going to change the subject in a minute if this is all just getting too intense – although Jesus was killed, he came back to life, and then instead of dying for a second time, he rose into heaven.* He's alive now, and it's possible to know him.

Yes, this is pretty wacky. But if you're prepared to go with the idea that – as a lot of historical evidence suggests – Jesus came back from the dead three days after being buried, then it's not too much of a stretch to imagine that the next step was equally supernatural. Plus, there's an awful lot of wacky stuff in everyday life that we never even question: the precise location of earth meaning it can support life at all; cats being terrified of cucumbers, and the continued popularity of TV gameshows. Just because it doesn't make sense, doesn't mean it's not real.

What does it actually mean to 'know' Jesus? Because that's not meant as a figure of speech; Christians literally believe that it's possible to have friendship and even conversation with God. As that sounds a bit weird, I think I can only explain it as I have experienced it. Since my mid teens, I've tried to follow Jesus as my role model, and my God. I get to know what he's like by reading about him, going to church and listening to wise people talk about him, and through talking with friends who know him too. Then when I'm on my own, I pray: I find somewhere quiet and talk to him (or into the air, or into my thoughts, in the belief he'll hear me) about every aspect of my life. I express gratitude for the good and sadness for the bad. I tell him about the things I'd love to see change, both within me and in my world. And then I try to make myself aware of how he might be talking back.

Now this is without doubt one of the most frustrating aspects of following Jesus. Not only is he invisible,* he's also very, very quiet. But while I do believe I've heard God speak out loud a couple of times in my life (to put that in context, that's about once every eight years), I think I've heard him many more times through the way my thoughts have been guided, through the wise words of others, through the apparent coincidences that have happened around me, and more. I firmly believe that God speaks, but that he chooses to do that in a wide variety of different ways.

At least, he's invisible in the sense that you can't see a first-century Middle-Eastern guy floating around your living room. But the Bible makes the excellent point that God reveals himself clearly by how incredible his creation is. For millennia, people have looked at mountains, lakes, canyons and forests and thought: ah, someone must have made that.

This ability to know Jesus, as well as just know about him, is important because – let's be honest – he's a hard act to follow. Incredibly wise, full of great character, compassionate and kind, and most importantly, perfect. Not only does he want us to follow his example, he wants to help us do it. So we don't simply read about Jesus and try to be like him, we can actually ask him to make us more like him. And of course, his example is unattainable, but that doesn't mean we shouldn't try to be at least somewhat like him. A man who is a less-than-perfect imitation of Jesus can still be a pretty fantastic man.

So this is a good moment to ask you: Does Jesus feel like a good role model? A great example to follow? Here are some more questions.

Think about . . .

Who are some of your role models? Sports stars, actors, musicians, maybe even politicians or other leaders?

What is it that you admire about them? What are the parts of them that you might even want to imitate?

Are you aware of their weaknesses or flaws? What *wouldn't* you want to imitate about them?

Why do you think Jesus was, and is, a role model to so many people?

What about Jesus do you think you would want to imitate?

Is there anything about Jesus' character that you don't think you'd want to copy?

What's one thing you could change or do to become a little more like Jesus?

Everything we've been talking about so far is the stuff of foundations – like the tons of concrete and other stuff that they put under a house when they're building it, to make sure it doesn't slip around or collapse. Your identity, character, sense of purpose and ideas about the sort of person you want to be or be like; these are the things that mark out who you really are.

Once those things are in place, the great news is that a lot of the hard work is done. And let's be honest: if you really have thought through those things, you're ahead of most people. What gets built on top – the actual house if you like – is the life you now choose to live. So for the rest of the book, we're going to look in detail at what building that house looks like. You've figured out who this guy is, and who you want him to be . . . now we're going to look at what it actually means to live everyday life as him.

4.
Feels:
a chapter
about
emotions

Boys don't cry.

We've talked a lot already about the stereotypical messaging we hear about girls; cheap-shot ideas about how they can't throw, or the jobs they can't do, or the sports they can't play. Generally speaking, the conversation around gender is about how men diminish women, and after thousands of years of male-dominated cultures, that seems fair enough. But the stereotypes around gender aren't just damaging for women; they also have an impact on us. And here's perhaps the most dangerous one of them all: the idea that emotion is feminine.

You probably know exactly what I'm talking about. As a boy, when you fell over in the playground, it's likely that you were given a quick hug and dust down, and then told to 'run it off'; while you saw girls in the same situation picked up, held and comforted. As a teenager, you'll have been expected to laugh through pain – both physical and psychological. You'd have understood from fairly early on that for men, emotion is repressed rather than displayed; bottled up, not let out.

You've almost certainly, at some point or other, been told to 'man up'. That's another tiny little phrase that packs a devastating punch. In five letters, it communicates in a nutshell the whole idea: that to be a man means putting aside tears, emotion, the experience of pain. It means gritting your teeth and moving on. It means neglecting your feelings and even your physical wounds, and drawing on some invisible secret reserve of man-power to move past whatever obstacle has come across your path.

But here's the problem: there is no invisible secret reserve of man-power. Not really, not in the long term.

What do you imagine might be the leading cause of death among young men in England and Wales between the ages of 20 and 49? Cancer maybe? Road accidents? Deaths linked to alcohol and drug abuse?

It's none of those. The leading cause of death among young men in England and Wales is suicide. The main reason young men die is because they have given up hope in life. Their negative emotions have spiralled to such a devastating extent that they believe the world around them will be better off without them in it. And this isn't just a British phenomenon; it's true across the world. Even in the USA, where guns are everywhere and their use is out of control, it's the second biggest cause of death in young men.

Yes, sadly many people of both sexes struggle with their mental health, and suicide can be a tragic end to that story for too many of them. Yet this isn't just a human thing, it's statistically also a male-dominated problem: young men are up to four times more likely to successfully commit suicide than young women. There's something about modern masculinity that ultimately makes it much more self-destructive.

Male suicide is ultimately what happens when a man believes he has run out of options; when, having suppressed his feelings for so long, he is suddenly overwhelmed by them. It is arguably the worst-case scenario when a man realizes he can't just 'man up' any longer. Considering and attempting suicide is the most serious mental health issue, and the stats seem to show that male brains are being pushed towards it much more often than female ones.

What seems clear, then, is that the idea that boys don't cry, that men don't experience or display emotion, isn't just dangerous but potentially lethal. Join the dots and we can clearly see that cultural ideas about repressed male emotion, which then become enacted by each passing generation of young men, are setting far too many of us up for a mental health crisis that could end in our deaths. That's how serious this is. That's how important it is that we delete 'man up' from our collective vocabularies.

Despite all the subtle messages we receive and then repeat about men and emotion, there are places where our natural desire to express emotion find a socially acceptable outlet. One of the most obvious and interesting examples of this is the sports field – a place where many men channel their interest. Just look at football (or, as my American friends may want to incorrectly call it, soccer*): for most of the game the players skulk around the pitch looking moody and barging into one another like animals jostling for territorial control. But then, when a goal is scored, the rules completely change. Not only is everyone all smiles, but there's widespread hugging, kissing, tears, and even the occasional dance routine. It's like the ban on emotional expression has temporarily been lifted.

*I know this is hardly the place, but it's football. American 'football' with all the pads and the adverts is mis-named and it's just time we all admitted it. Those guys barely kick the ball; let's just agree to rename it 'Throwball' or 'Fancy Dress Rugby' and the world can move on.

If it's suddenly emotional on the pitch, that's nothing compared to what's going on in the watching stands. Men who normally can't even look one another in the eye when talking are hugging and jumping around together arm in arm. Tears run down their cheeks as they celebrate the concentrated jolt of joy that the goal has delivered. At the other end of the stadium, an equivalent amount of negative emotion is being released as guys console one another, vent their feelings of devastation at the heavens, and in some cases, allow the tears of disappointment and punctured dreams to flow freely.

A lot of people express disdain for the way men – and women, who also make up a significant section of any football crowd – get so emotionally involved in a game, when these same people can struggle to show anywhere near the same level of concern or connection to seemingly more important things. In fact, I think it should be seen as a huge positive that these men actually find an outlet for their emotions, because it seems to me that the moment this kind of emotional release is 'allowed', it's immediately and gladly expressed. Physical contact, bonding over a common cause, sharing a moment together with others, removing the mask and allowing them to see your vulnerabilities: these are all things that men and women desperately need – and if supporting a football team enables that, surely it can't be a bad thing.

What arguably isn't so positive is the fact that for many men, this is where allowed emotion starts and ends. That beyond the strange collective safety of the sports ground, feelings are once again bottled and repressed. Men don't generally hug one another at the beginning and end of the working day, or let out little tears of joy when they see a friend. Sport seems to be very much the exception rather than the rule. That means that while there are some positive spaces in a man's life where he's allowed to let the cork out of the bottle, for the most part we're all still subscribing to the idea that men don't really 'do' emotion, that boys don't cry.

I am increasingly finding myself faced with the unnerving reality of my own aging. Weird hairs are beginning to sprout from my ears, and I'm often finding myself drawn to classical and jazz music.

It's obviously a little while since I went through my own formative years – the time in my life when I learned that men aren't meant to show emotion – but because the world has moved on, I had assumed that things were probably changing. After all, the idea of what a 'real man' is has been slowly disassembled by the media. Our movies now include a more varied group of male heroes – the world now has both an intellectual Doctor Strange and a ripped Aquaman – and many of the old gender stereotypes are being deleted from music and television. YouTubers, who don't have to play by any rules set by their elder generation (because there wasn't one), don't set out to reinforce those old ideas. My assumption, then, was that young men would no longer be growing up with such a sense that emotion is female, and that men shouldn't feel – or express feelings – in the same way.

I may be old, but I still spend a large chunk of my life working with teenagers.* Recently I found myself sitting with a group of 14- and 15-year-old guys leading a discussion around this subject. What surprised me (although perhaps it shouldn't have) was how clearly they still perceived the idea that men don't 'do' emotion. One of them actually said 'we're not meant to show feelings, are we?' Despite all the positive messages in the media to the contrary, this guy – a popular, kind, well-adjusted 14-year-old – had absorbed the overriding idea that men hide emotions. As we worked our way around the group, each of these young men agreed that this was their perception of gender and emotion. 'Girls are more emotional,' said one. 'Guys bottle it up,' said another. And while there was a general sense in the group that this wasn't entirely healthy, there was a broad acceptance that it was just the way things will always be.

Some people might say I need to grow up and move on. I don't. I think teenagers are pretty much the most exciting people on the planet. So much hope, so much creativity, so much determination to change the world for the better. They're just . . . amazing little balls of potential (which coincidentally, was the original title of this book).

I don't think it's scaremongering to suggest that if these attitudes don't change, then neither will those tragic suicide statistics. The fact that men feel ill-equipped to express, and even forbidden from expressing, their emotions is not just something we should accept.

You were created to feel. The human brain is designed to process a whole range of emotions, and due to a mix of hormones, thoughts and external influences, you're naturally going to feel most or all of them. Some of them feel good: things like happiness, joy and pride.* Others don't feel good: but still have an important place: emotions like fear, sadness, anger and disgust. Then there are wildcards like surprise, which can go either way. The brain (and in some cases, the rest of the body) feels all of these things for good reason, and that's why bottling them up and suppressing them is not a good idea.

*You know, the nice kind of pride. The other day my son Samuel scored a goal from inside his own half of the football pitch. All the other kids jumped on him because eight-year-old boys don't care about how much emotion they show. My heart swelled in my chest, although it's worth noting that I also feel a tinge of sadness about the fact that by the age of eight Samuel has already scored about 15 more competitive goals than I did in my entire playing 'career'. The other kind of pride, the arrogant kind, is not so positive.

It might surprise you to know that Jesus – the great role model – experienced and expressed a full range of human emotions. Again, we often just don't think of him like that,* as having had the same kinds of feelings we do. I think we instinctively imagine him to be somehow above all that, drifting around with an entirely balanced and healthy mind at all times, unencumbered by any strong emotion. That doesn't really add up though: if he was fully human, he felt it all. And the Bible backs that up too – in various stories we see him demonstrating lots of different feelings.

I think in our minds Jesus is more like one of those old Action Man dolls with no private parts. Except, you know, in an emotional sense. This is wrong. I also don't think he had a string in his back that you could pull to get him to say one of five set phrases, nor did he have a karate-chop action.

As we saw in the previous chapter, Jesus got seriously angry on at least one memorable occasion. And it's important to repeat that the release of anger wasn't a bad thing in itself; it was motivated by his disgust (another emotion) for the way the Temple was being abused by greedy people. It's likely that Jesus felt angry and disgusted at other points too – after all, we only have detailed records of a relatively small part of his life – and we can suppose that these emotions often came out in response to the unkindness and unfairness he saw around him in the fairly brutal ancient world.

We also looked at how Jesus reacted with coolness and compassion when his friends tried to defend him against his betrayers. But just before that bit with the whole ear disappear/reappear trick, Jesus is praying alone in that garden I mentioned, and we see perhaps the most extreme example of his emotional vulnerability on display. In the Gospel of Luke, Jesus is described as being 'in anguish' as he contemplates the torturous death he's about to endure. That's perhaps understandable – how would any of us feel if we knew that not only were we about to be led away to death, but that this would come through the betrayal of a close friend? But then Luke adds something extraordinary: he says '[Jesus'] sweat was like drops of blood falling to the ground' (Luke 22.44).

Many people think that this wasn't just a figure of speech, but the description of a real medical phenomenon. There's an unusual condition called hematohidrosis, which is where – in moments of extreme anxiety – one's sweat can contain blood, taken from the tiny blood vessels that surround our sweat glands. Luke, who wrote these words, was a physician himself, so he might well have understood something about this. But regardless of whether this was more literal or metaphorical, it's clear that Jesus experienced some very strong, very dark feelings in this moment. It's another little reminder that whatever we're going through, he's been through it too.

Jesus didn't only experience difficult or painful emotions however. There's another bit in Luke* where we read that Jesus was full of 'joy' – not a word we tend to use, but one that means extreme happiness. While we might have Jesus pegged as a serious man, his storytelling style suggests he was a pretty good-humoured guy. He made quite a lot of jokes of the 'you had to be there' variety, which don't translate today but would have had people rolling around in AD 30. He certainly wasn't characterized by sadness or anxiety.

*The reference, if you're interested, is Luke 10.21. In fact, the original Greek language in which Luke wrote uses a phrase which is more like 'jumping for joy'. Imagine Jesus with two feet off the ground, punching the air, like a guy in a motivational business poster.

That said, Jesus did notably disprove the idea that boys don't cry. There's a story in which word reaches him that one of his best friends is sick. This man, called Lazarus, gets very seriously ill while Jesus is off preaching in another part of the country, but Jesus decides to stay where he is for another two days before visiting his friend. In the time that he is away, Lazarus's condition worsens and eventually it kills him. When Jesus realizes that his friend is dead, he travels to where the body is buried and famously turns him into a zombie (or, you know, just brings him back to life). Before that though, we get John 11.35, the shortest verse in the entire Bible: 'Jesus wept.' Even though he knows he's got the power to resurrect his friend, Jesus still instinctively cries. Interestingly, this doesn't happen when Jesus first learns of Lazarus's death, but when he's actually standing at the mouth of his tomb. This isn't a cold, rational reaction, it's an emotional one. It happens because Jesus is a human being, who loves his friend and feels the pain of his loss in that moment like a knife to the heart.

At some point in history, the people who divided the modern Bible into chapters and verses decided to separate those two words off all on their own, and I think they did so for a reason. This statement is incredible when you think about it: Jesus, who was actually God in human form, cried real tears over the death of one single person – even one he could then save. This is significant; it's important. Jesus doesn't just care about people but about every individual person, you and I included. He loved Lazarus – the people watching on say as much – and he loves us. His capacity to express and feel love was and is enormous.

Part of what made Jesus so able to express that love was the fact that he allowed his emotions to show. He didn't bottle up his feelings, he expressed them. He loved his friend, so he cried; he felt anger at injustice, so he fought back; he felt great anguish, so he cried out to God. In a culture of bottled-up male emotions, Jesus is a breath of fresh air: a blueprint for a healthier kind of masculinity.

I'm not suggesting that men should look for every opportunity to cry. Tears are not the only outlet for emotion, and you can be in touch with your feelings without having to burst into them. Nor am I advocating for every man to become a 'sensitive type', if that's not naturally who you are. But becoming aware of your feelings, and understanding that they're normal and valid – whatever the world might say – is vital. It's OK to feel, and it's OK to talk about how we feel. In fact, it's potentially life-saving.

Managing and processing our feelings properly is a big part of our mental health and emotional well-being. Again, this isn't something that we're particularly good at thinking about. Historically, this has been a part of human welfare that has been neglected across both sexes; people with broken legs will be treated with concern and compassion, while those with depression can frequently be told: 'Pull yourself together.' Thankfully more and more people are taking this side of health more seriously, but again, this still seems to be less true among men.

A lot of men are very good at looking after their physical health. Near where I live, the most popular fitness classes are military-based; people with far too much money on their hands part with a large monthly fee for the privilege of having a retired soldier shout at them to 'hit the deck and give me 20'. Sometimes I like to sit and watch them while eating a sausage roll. Male participation in these sessions is high, and a lot of men seem to derive a bizarre amount of enjoyment from being barked at and throwing themselves in muddy puddles (which incidentally is also how my dog likes to spend her free time). Anyway, they seem to love it, and they also end up looking impressively buff as a result.

If military fitness isn't your thing then perhaps you run, or swim, or play a team sport, or go to the gym. There are plenty of exceptions, but men tend to try to take care of their physical health. The same is not generally true of our emotional health. We don't tend to put anywhere near as much care into our brains as we do into our hearts. In fact, most of us don't even think about doing so. Yet while physical exercise is one really important factor in maintaining a healthy state of mind, there are plenty of others too, and by default we neglect them.

Sleep is really important. If you're reading this in your teens, you may well have no argument with this, but it's incredible how quickly sleep becomes sacrificed, especially when it becomes involved in a contest with either entertainment or ambition. We all love sleep, but we're also all part of an always-on culture that gives us plenty of reasons to stay awake. Whether it's one more Netflix episode or waking up intermittently to read your notifications, our desire to sleep is continually attacked by distraction and FOMO;* our device-addicted brains trick us into believing that the alternative – being asleep – is boring and unnecessary. We think we can cope just fine with less, but by tiring out our brains, we're making them less healthy. And once we begin to throw ourselves into work and career, we tell ourselves the same lie: that we can cut corners and win ourselves some extra waking hours, as if doing so will give us some sort of competitive edge. Maybe it will for a time, but when times of stress come, we'll try to face them with brains that have been starved of rest. We need to sleep, and never to allow ourselves to see unconscious time as wasted time.

*Apparently at time of writing this means 'Fear Of Missing Out'. By the time you read this, it might mean something completely different, like 'Fear Of Mr Orange', or 'Fart On My Own'. Language is funny. Funnier than me, it seems.

Spending time with friends – in real life, not just virtually – is another important component of good emotional health. Sometimes when we're not feeling so good, we can have a tendency to shut ourselves away from other people, when actually social interaction is likely to make us feel better. Again, this might not seem like a difficult thing to do, but with so much 'friendship' now taking place virtually, it can be easy to neglect face-to-face contact.

Connected to this, it's also healthy to take regular breaks from your phone, and from social media, for the sake of keeping a good perspective. If we're not careful, we can become absorbed in a world of 'liking' other people's photos and comments, and then obsessing over why no one has 'liked' ours. We'll look at this in more detail in another chapter, but social media plays tricks with the chemicals in our brain, to the point that we start to derive our mood from our feelings of online popularity. So take breaks, and own your phone; don't let your phone own you.

It is, however, really good and positive to have fun, relax and embrace interests and the things that you find entertaining. When my eldest son Joel started secondary school, I was staggered at how much homework he received each week; an amount that seems to grow steadily each year. I'm reliably informed that this is normal: that most young people have a couple of hours of work to do at the end of every school day, and all I can say if you're currently at that stage of life is that I empathize, and that adult life is quite a lot easier. But if our culture has decided that this level of work pressure is normal and healthy, then it makes the time we spend recharging our spent batteries even more precious.

Just as we're attracted back time and again to junk foods that we know aren't good for us, it's easy to slip into comfortable but unsatisfying patterns of rest. Instead of investing ourselves into activities that we know are really enjoyable but require a bit of effort, we drift time and again towards the lowest common denominator. Instead of going for a run, we watch TV; instead of cooking a delicious meal for ourselves, we microwave something and then play *Call of Duty*. We don't even do the relatively easy stuff well: when we sit down to apparently give our full attention to a movie we love, we actually only have half an eye on it while scrolling through Instagram.

Here's my weakness: I love to read books, and derive great pleasure once I'm absorbed in a good novel – but I never seem to get one open. Instead, I have an addiction to repetitive smartphone games. For a while it was *Candy Crush Saga*, and after that it was *Toon Blast*.* It seems I can't get enough of simple, colour-matching puzzle games, but I dread to think how many great works of English literature I could have read in the time it's taken me to get to level 2401 of an ultimately pointless game.

I know, I know. This is pathetic. Quite apart from lacking the self-control to delete these ridiculous apps from my phone, I'm also displaying horrendously poor taste in video games. Where's the variety? Where's the innovation? Nope – I just like lining up coloured blocks in a row, over and over again.

Not all rest is healthy, or even restful. Just because the thing you're doing isn't work, or isn't hard, doesn't mean it's actually replenishing your reserves of energy and concentration. Apart from the frustrating sense of wasted time, these junk-rest activities don't build us up in any way. Sitting down to write or paint releases creativity; listening to music or watching great cinema inspires our imagination; going for a walk surrounded by nature gives us a sense of peace and space for our thoughts to unwind a bit. This is the kind of rest that actually puts something back into the space that hard work and stress have emptied out.

There's a bit in the Bible where Jesus is starting to reach the heights of mass popularity, and you can imagine his head is absolutely full to bursting. His name is spreading like wildfire; he's now in charge of leading a group of guys around and showing them how to live. Everywhere he goes he's expected to say incredibly wise things and perform miraculous signs. He's fast becoming a bit of a celebrity, at least in the local area, and he's probably absolutely exhausted. And in one particular story, which concerns him healing a man with a terrible disease,* the Bible says something really startling about how Jesus chooses to process all this attention, pressure and stress. If you or I found that our popularity was growing like that of a YouTuber whose kitten video just went unexpectedly viral, we'd probably embrace our moment of fame. But Jesus does something else – it says he withdraws to a lonely place, to pray. Even as he's becoming more and more famous and sought after, he goes into hiding and spends time praying. What's more, the text actually says he 'often' did this, as if his primary way of dealing with the pressures of being the highly publicized Son of God was to get away from people, and reconnect with his Father.

The story can be found in Luke chapter 5. Jesus specifically tells the man not to tell anyone about what's happened, because he's trying to keep a lid on it; grow his movement slowly. This doesn't happen at all – news spreads fast and even more crowds flock. I imagine the man agreed to Jesus' request and then instantly ran to tell everyone he'd ever met, like a guy you just confided in about your really embarrassing rash. Wouldn't you do the same thing if you met the Son of God?

It might seem a bit weird to think that Jesus, who was himself God, took time out to pray. For him, though, this was simply about spending time with his Father, talking with him about the life he was living on earth at the time, and in a sense it's no different for us. I think Jesus knew the power of prayer to rebuild people when they're tired out and spent. He knew the value of taking time to ask God for help, and to listen for his voice. He felt restored and replenished by this activity, and he got the most out of it by retreating to a quiet place. If your head is feeling full, prayer can genuinely help as you try to make sense of things.

Prayer is also something that can help if you find yourself in a dark or desperate place. Talking to the God who loves you can create a tremendous sense of reassurance, and he often brings a sense of comfort to those who seek him in distress. If you do find yourself in that kind of place, however – and I can't stress this enough – you should also talk to another person about it. To a family member if appropriate, or to someone else you trust. Sometimes our feelings can be overwhelming, and none of us need suffer those moments on our own.

Good emotional health is yet another level of foundation on which to build your life as a man. Our ability to form and maintain relationships is hugely influenced by it, as is our capability to carve out and grow a career. So often it's the part of a man's life that gets the least attention; in fact, it's vitally important. Before you go any further, take a few moments to consider whether your emotional health needs a bit more thought.

Think about . . .

How good are you at expressing the things you feel? Whom do you feel comfortable sharing your emotions with?

To what degree do you bottle up your feelings? How do you intend to process those feelings in the long term?

What coping mechanisms do you use if and when you feel overwhelmed by feelings? How well do these mechanisms work for you?

What healthy habits do you have at the moment to ensure you're looking after your mental and emotional health? Is it something you ever consider?

How helpful do you find it to pray through your thoughts and feelings?

What one change could you make to your lifestyle that would improve your emotional health?

Forget what the stereotype says. You were made with feelings and emotions, and the most fulfilling version of your life is the one in which you let them all exist in their proper places. Allow yourself to love deeply, to cry if you feel the need to release some emotion, to get angry at the right times and joyful when things go right. There is no better example of masculinity than that of Jesus, who did all of the above and is still widely regarded as the greatest man who ever lived.

5.
Lines:
a chapter
about
sex

This is the sex chapter.

I'm putting that piece of information up front because I imagine it will be extremely helpful for you if you're scanning through these pages looking for it. I could make a desperate case for the other 90 per cent of the book – which will look at all the other important elements of life as a man *apart* from sex – but I'm not going to patronize you. If you're reaching this point after sequentially reading the first half of the book, congratulations for making it through so many of my stories. If you're joining us at this point – welcome!

Whoever you are, I would imagine that this is the one topic you most want to read about, but probably the one that you least enjoy talking about. Unless you're one of those awful people who makes everyone else uncomfortable by discussing the contents of their trousers at the dinner table, this is likely to be something that you think about in private. And boy, do you think about it a lot . . .

There has been a *lot* of harmful Christian teaching on sex and relationships; teaching that has damaged people, filled them with shame, pushed them away from God and hurt their ability to conduct healthy relationships. I know that, because 25 years ago or so, I was on the receiving end of some of it. In my teenage years I went to a lot of talks about sex and relationships at Christian conferences, and some of the stuff I heard there really messed up my head. I remember weird catchphrases like 'don't touch what you haven't got',* and 'always keep one foot on the floor' (a bizarre attempt to stop young people having sex which just invited creativity and invention). The main idea was that sex before marriage was bad – no, shameful – and that it made God angry with you. Once you'd had sex and lost your virginity, you couldn't go back; in doing so you had ruined your sexual future, and maybe left God forever disappointed with you too.

This is still my best defence for why I developed man-boobs. It also doesn't really make sense when you think about it: most of the erogenous zones are common to both sexes, and this phrase doesn't exactly help people who are same-sex attracted.

Actually, I heard worse stuff than that. There was a strange phrase that someone invented a few years ago, which spiritualized the whole thing to a dangerous level: the concept of a 'soul tie'. The idea was that when you had sex with someone and became what the Bible calls 'one flesh' (I know, it sounds like something out of *Fifty Shades of Grey*, but it's in the Bible), you created a link between your two souls. Someone who'd had lots of sexual partners, it followed, had created a whole load of ties to the souls of those other people. Their soul was a tangled mess, and on a spiritual level this was very bad news. I cannot emphasize this strongly enough, partly because my lovely publisher won't let me. This is absolute, total, dangerously stupid nonsense. This is not in the Bible. God never said this; Jesus never gave a sermon on a rock in first-century Palestine about the danger of soul ties. It was invented as a way of spiritualizing the dangers of sexual promiscuity, and because it's such a deep and weighty idea, it messes people up.

I hope you've never heard that particular youth talk, but even if you haven't, I'm sure you recognize the Church's somewhat overzealous and weirdly obsessive attitude to sex. If you ask the average person in the street what Christians care about, I'm fairly certain sex will be near the very top of their list. Sex, promiscuity, masturbation – they've all risen to the summit of things the Church loudly prohibits – far above things like greed, selfishness and allowing millions of children to live in poverty.

The language that's sometimes used by Christians on this subject is incredibly powerful – and not in a good way. It's the language of 'purity' and 'failure'; 'clean' and 'dirty'. Words can have a powerful impact on our sense of self-worth, and these words in particular can either create a fragile anxiety about not upsetting God, or a profound feeling of guilt, shame and unworthiness. Far too many people gave up on the Church because they made a decision to sleep with someone and were made to feel disgusting as a result.

Now, before you think I'm about to hand you a free pass to sleep with anyone you want, I'm really not. The way that this subject has been addressed and taught by Christians over the years is horribly flawed . . . but some of the principles are right. There's no such thing as soul ties; there's no point expecting someone to remember a set of corny phrases and remain abstinent as a result. God doesn't want people to feel ashamed – that's precisely why he sent Jesus into the world. But that doesn't mean he doesn't care about your love life. He does. Because sex is an incredible, glorious thing. Of course it is – why else would we all want it so much? And when I say glorious, I mean it in the spiritual, heaven-sent sense. Sex is God's invention, given to us as a gift so that we can enjoy intense pleasure and total intimacy with another person all at the same time. God created sex deliberately; that's why it's so good, and that's why he cares how we use it.

At which point – excruciatingly, given that my own children might at some point read this – I'm going to talk about my own sex life. From a cultural perspective, there's very little to tell. When I was 19, I met Jo, the love of my life; I'd had a few relationships beforehand with very nice girls but they'd never become sexual. Jo and I dated for five years and married, and over that time we never had sex. Now, as I've already admitted, part of that was down to some pretty overbearing Christian teaching we'd both received, but at least I have the benefit of knowing what it looks like to wait. We had sex for the first time on our wedding night, and that's 100 per cent the honest truth.

(A brief detour at this point, just to emphasize what an idiot I am. Many people pretend not to be having sex while they're growing up; I did the opposite. When I arrived at university and made friends, I was slightly intimidated by the fact that everyone else seemed to have a catalogue of past sexual partners by the age of 18. So, in freshers' week, when my friend Jamie asked me how many girls I'd slept with, I blurted out 'five!', and then had to fabricate a list of exciting one-night stands. This was not only stupid, it was also a time bomb: as soon as my friends from home and my friends from university had a chance to meet a few weeks later, it went off almost instantly and I was exposed as a prat.)

Anyway, despite the intimidating and rather dangerous teaching I received about sex, I'm incredibly glad that as a result I didn't sleep with anyone else before my wife. I'm glad that she doesn't have to imagine the thought of me doing incredibly intimate things with a host of other people; I'm glad I don't have memories of sex with other women to somehow compare against sex with her. Much, much more than that though, with the benefit of a lot of hindsight, I'm glad that the level of closeness and intimacy that sex brings is something that I've only had within the context of our relationship. It's especially special because it's ours and only ours. And I think, 16 years into marriage at time of writing, that I understand why all those Christians – however misguided their way of telling us might have been - thought sex was intended for the context of one relationship.

As I mentioned a moment ago, the Bible talks about men and women leaving their parents behind and joining together as 'one flesh'. Sex is a key part of the bond which – rather literally when you think about it – joins and glues a relationship together. That's obviously what drives the 'soul tie' idea, but I think the people who teach it just have the wrong emphasis. Sex doesn't tie our souls – because, let's face it, this isn't *Dungeons & Dragons* – but it's a beautiful and practical way to deepen a relationship so much that you can imagine spending the rest of your lives together sharing a home, a name and maybe a family. As we become 'one flesh', we become a single unit ready to take on the world.

Which means that sex is special, rather than dirty. Worth saving for the right person, rather than forbidden until marriage. I didn't have sex because I was scared of messing up and making God angry; I wish I'd not had sex because I had such a sense of perspect-ive that I was prepared to save sexual intimacy for the person with whom I was going to have the adventure of a lifetime. Right decision, wrong reasons.

The trouble with all of this admirable high thinking, however, is the contents of a man's trousers. Or more accurately, the mix of chemicals constantly whirring around his brain which make him instinctively keen to enjoy as much sexual activity as possible, and which frequently translates to his trousers. I am not saying any of this without a huge awareness of how difficult this is; the human brain, and especially the male teenage brain, is fighting very hard to get you to respond to sexual desire. If you're going to somehow stop yourself from doing so, then you're in for the fight of your life. I know this, because I myself have trousers.

Most men think about sex – or rather, they're reminded of how attractive other people are, and how that makes them feel – often. Very often in fact. When you're a teenage boy, however, you've got hormonal rushes constantly amplifying the whole thing. Your brain is suddenly wired with attraction to people you previously thought were just annoying; you're prone to big emotional swings, so that the person you slightly fancy feels like the undying love of your life. And of course, there's a very physical complication: the rushes of blood to a certain part of your anatomy which seems to happen regularly, rapidly and without warning.

You're on a bus – potentially one that doesn't even contain anyone that you're remotely attracted to – and you're aware that the blood has started rushing *there* for no apparent reason. Or perhaps there's more of a direct link; you're kissing someone, and within a nano-second you're having to angle your body backwards so as not to appear as subtle as a randy dog. Penises are a pain when you're growing up, and the fact that they can become activated faster than the Avengers does not help if you're trying to navigate your teenage years without having sex.

This problem is compounded by the fact that sex is everywhere in our culture. In advertising, it's used to sell everything from car tyres to peanuts; a recent ad for toothpaste aimed at university students was designed to look like a shot from a porn video. In music, it's often the mechanism by which big stars – both male and female – try to get an edge; videos are filled with erotic images and people wearing very little. It's discussed in magazines and TV shows as the ultimate recreational pastime, as if finding someone to have sex with is just a bit like finding a running partner. And underpinning all of this, pouring fuel into the fire of sexual obsession within our culture, is pornography.

I'm going to talk more about porn in the next chapter, but it needs a mention here. The link between the free accessibility of hardcore pornography, and increasingly disposable, so-called liberated attitudes towards sex cannot be overstated. Before the arrival of high-speed Internet, and particularly of secretive portable devices on which to access it, porn was a relatively small business. In order to look at pictures of naked people, you would need to embrace the almost indescribable awkwardness of facing up to a newsagent and handing him a copy of a printed magazine.*

I mean, can you imagine how hideous that would be? You would have to walk into a shop – possibly one where local people would be; people who might know your parents. You'd have to stand on tiptoe to reach the top shelf, and unless you were actually going to spend time browsing, snatch a copy of a magazine which would have a cover with less subtlety than a car alarm, and then take it to the counter. At which point, you would need to interact with another human being, and pay them for something which you both knew you were about to go home and masturbate over. How many people would look at porn if that was the only way you could get it? This was the actual reality for teenagers from about 1970 to 2000.

If you actually wanted to watch people having sex with each other on video, you would need to venture even further into the murky underbelly of society, and somehow visit a sex shop – convincing the owner that you were over the age of 18. Now granted, most people my age saw a porn film when we were growing up because you went to a friend's house and their older brother thought it would be funny to corrupt you; but very few guys in my generation owned or viewed porn films on their own.

Now of course, porn is freely available everywhere, all the time. I'm not going to patronize you by suggesting that you might not know how to access it – although if you don't, I'm delighted for you, and please seek it out only as you might try to find a vial of anthrax. What's happened as a result of this availability is that porn has become *normalized*, and that's a problem for all sorts of reasons.

One of those reasons is that porn has cheapened sex. In a world where everyone is watching porn, sex has come to be seen as a recreational activity between any two (or three, or more) people. Ripped out of the context for which it was intended, it becomes as profound as a game of table tennis, or a round of bingo. Porn says: anyone can do anything with anyone, at any time, in any way. There are no consequences, and there's no need for anything as sentimental as love or even romance. Porn reduces sex to an animalistic, almost random encounter that can happen without any sort of build-up, and with zero meaning attached.

It seems to me that on some level, that's where our culture's attitude to sex is heading. If it feels good, and you don't get hurt, then do whatever you like, with whoever you like. Some people call that liberation. I don't. Because porn lies.

Porn says sex is like *this*, but anyone who's ever had sex knows that it isn't.

Porn says look at these people enjoying themselves . . . but there's a catalogue of former porn stars who wish they'd never done it; women who claim they had to be high on class A drugs just to get through the shoots, people who are so shattered by the experience that they've been unable to have relationships or even build a life afterwards.

Porn says sex has no consequences, but porn actors have contracted AIDS and other diseases, or developed drug addictions or mental health issues, as a direct result of their participation in the industry.

Porn says sex is about gratification, rather than mutual pleasure.

Porn says violence – particularly male violence against women – is OK and a part of a normal sexual experience.

Porn says sex is throwaway, disposable, meaningless.

Porn lies. And because of the influence that those lies are having on our culture, the average person's view of sex can become seriously warped out of shape. Because deep down – by instinct – we know these things aren't right.

The truth is that sex is incredibly meaningful, and I believe that the biggest reason why is that it's *holy*. It's not just a physical action but it's also a spiritual experience, designed by God as a gift to us. When we have sex with someone, we experience perhaps the closest form of intimacy that it's possible to achieve; we are literally joined together with another person. It's incredibly special, and in spite of all the pressure that a sex-mad culture might want to apply, it's worth reserving for someone we truly love.

I imagine – having had no experience – that sex without love is alright. You go through the motions, you derive a certain amount of satisfaction, you move on. But actually, sex is *nothing like* those things because you can't just experience the highest possible level of intimacy, and just move on. It just doesn't work like that, because it's not a mechanical process (another lie that porn will try to tell you). You can't detach your head and heart; sex remains meaningful even when you don't want it to.

Right now, mentally at least, you may agree with the idea that sex shouldn't be anywhere near as cheap and throwaway as our culture seems to suggest. But still, it's really, really difficult to turn that intellectual agreement into action. Sex is everywhere in the media, porn is casting a huge shadow, and then there's the small matter of peer pressure, or: *everyone else is doing it, so why shouldn't I?*

Here's what it comes down to: being a man who decides not to have sex doesn't mean setting yourself against the wind; it means staring down a hurricane. Everything around you is going to tell you that the thing your hormone-charged body is urging you to do is good and healthy and for *right now*. If you're going to stand up against that, then you're going to need to find some pretty deep wells of strength, resilience and self-control.

The way you do that, of course, is by looking beyond yourself, and looking beyond the *right now*. That kind of perspective isn't easy, but it is possible. You are capable of saying no. You are capable of looking ahead to the future and saying that you want sex to be something that you save for the context of love and commitment. And that is so much easier if you're asking God for help; continually returning to him with brutal honesty and asking him to help you to stick to your principles, rather than surrender to your desires.

I think we imagine that God isn't really very keen on that sort of conversation. We probably imagine him to be a bit prudish, and almost offended by talk of our sexuality. But when we think like that, we forget that he designed the entire system. He invented penises and vaginas; he can cope with a bit of locker-room talk. God desires an utterly honest relationship with us, and being omniscient he has *quite literally* seen it all. He is not going to be shocked if you want to talk to him about how difficult you're finding it not to sleep with someone, in fact he deeply desires that you would talk to him about that sort of thing, rather than keeping it in some sort of secret compartment in the recesses of your brain.

If you want to face down the hurricane, you need God's help. And as difficult as it might be, it is possible. Don't let anyone tell you that it isn't. You do not have to have sex, just because everyone else seems to be. You can save sex for marriage, or at least for the most special of relationships, if you want to. That is your decision, and don't let anyone make you feel strange for making it.

Of course, it may be that all of this feels a bit late. It might be that you've already had sex, or that you're currently in a sexual relationship. These words may currently be filling you with frustration, guilt, sadness, rage or any combination thereof. If so, that's not my intention at all.

To return to those old youth talks I mentioned, I am sick of meeting people who have turned their back on God and the Church because they were made to feel shameful that they'd had sex. It is agonizing to meet men and women who made a decision on their future relationship with the almighty Creator of the universe because they were told they'd angered and disappointed him. Yet this is something that I hear far too often.

So let me be crystal clear: if you've already had sex, I do not believe that God is angry with you. I do not believe that you've messed up, or 'failed' sexually. But the choice to save sex is still before you, and it restarts today. Just because you've had sex, doesn't mean you can't stop having sex. Even if you're in a relationship that's become sexual, it doesn't follow that you can't stop that side of things without killing the rest.

In a sex-mad, everyone-is-doing-it culture, it can almost feel like the decision *not* to have sex – what some people call abstinence or celibacy – is out of our hands. But that's another lie. You can abstain from sex now, even if you've been having sex before, just like you can decide to wait if you haven't had sex already. And there are three really good reasons for this: 1) it says that you're not going to be controlled by a sex-mad, pornified culture; 2) it's an investment in the big, long-term relationship that you hope to have in the future; and 3), it's a profound statement of intent towards God.

God's desire is that his gift of sex is kept special. He wants us to enjoy it, but he doesn't want us to throw it around like the sort of gift that we don't care about. You know when you get birthday presents and they're of wildly different values? Someone gives you a smartwatch (I use this example of a great gift entirely in the hope that my wife might see it), and someone else gets you a cheap bit of plastic. You'd treat those gifts in very different ways, right? You wouldn't take much care of the random plastic nonsense, and you'd let anyone play with it. But the smartwatch you'd guard with your life. God's gift of sex is the smartwatch* in this example. It's precious, it has great personal value, and most importantly of all it communicates the love and care of the person who gave it to you.

Sex can't stream music, or tell you when you've got an incoming phone call. It will help you burn calories though.

How we treat sex reveals something about how we see God. Do we care about what he thinks about the gift he's given us, and how we use it? Again, this is not meant to make you feel guilty about how you've viewed sex in the past, but it is meant as an encouragement to take responsibility from now on. You get to choose if you're going to have sex – no one else.

Let's just say, for argument's sake, that you're now (perhaps a little reluctantly) convinced. How do you do relationships in *this* culture, without inevitably ending up in bed with each other? It might seem unrealistic, but I promise you it's possible.

For a start, a good question to ask is: why do I want to have a relationship with this person? Is it because I like them, I enjoy their company, and I like who I am around them? If so, these seem like excellent reasons to be in a relationship with someone. If this is why you want to be with someone, it also follows that you will want to treat them well and look after them. If, however, your starting point for your relationship is simply that you're attracted to this person and the way they look, it's more likely that your motivations for being with them are more selfish. That's not to say you shouldn't respond to attraction of course – but if that's the only real reason for being together, it's a pretty flawed relationship from the start. And if your relationship is really only based on attraction, and therefore what your hormones are saying, then you'll probably find it difficult not to respond to those hormones and their impulses.

If your relationship is founded on a surer footing – and you're actually great friends who are attracted to each other – then the urge to have sex becomes a smaller part of the bigger picture. It's easier to say no when there's so much more to your relationship than that. There are an awful lot of great bits to a good relationship – talking about nonsense until the small hours, having new experiences together, supporting one another, spending time with other people 'as a couple', and generally having fun. In the light of all these things, sex becomes just one other possible dimension to your relationship, and one that then becomes more realistic to wait for.

At this point you may be forming the great, age-old question about sex: so, how far is too far? Or to put it more candidly: how much am I allowed to get away with? The problem with this question is that it suggests that there's a set list of rules somewhere about sex. There isn't, not even in the Bible. It's up to us to decide how much of God's gift of sex we choose to unwrap early. A really important question to ask in response, though, is: why are you asking that? Is your desire to push those boundaries a bit further driven by your love for another person, or by your own gratification? Usually in truth it's more about the latter.

Ultimately, that's why most people have sex outside the context of a truly loving relationship: they want personal satisfaction. Again, that's a message that our culture has been feeding us for years: that you deserve to enjoy regular orgasms as part of being a human. But that's born out of a really flawed and broken view of the world: that life is all about what we can get out of it, rather than what we can contribute.

Sex is usually good. Of course it is: that's why it's one of the main driving forces even in our economy. Yet there's something so much better: sex within the context of love; it feels different, and it's ultimately way more satisfying – for both of you. That's the kind of sex that you were made for, and it was made as a gift for you.

In a world where sex is never far from the conversation, our decisions around it are a vital aspect of the kind of man we're deciding to be. As with so much else, refusing to make these kinds of decisions just means we'll be deciding by default to join in with the masses, and probably embrace a broken view of sex and relationships that's corrupted by porn and driven by money and a flawed version of liberation. So don't decide by default: think about how you want to use that gift of sex, and act intentionally as a result. Your future self might just thank you for it.

Think about . . .

How often do you think about sex? What do you do with those thoughts and feelings?

Do you think sex is worth waiting for? If not, why not? If so, what would you wait for?

How much do you access porn? How do you feel about it?

What makes a good relationship (apart from sex)? What are the most important things in a prospective partner?

What decisions do you want to make about sex and your future? Whom do you know whose attitude to sex and relationships you admire? Could you approach this person to ask him or her to help you think about some of this stuff?

On that last point, you might find it helpful to actually identify a role model: an older guy you are sure (or you think probably) handles sex and relationships with wisdom. If this is an area that you know you need some help with, then take the initiative and find someone who'll be up for talking openly about this subject, and will even hold you accountable to the decisions you tell him you want to make. If that feels like a really awkward conversation, then I give you full permission to blame me. Just say: 'Some guy in a book I've been reading said I should find an older role model to talk to me about sex.' There you go – instantly makes you look much less weird.

6.
Itches:
a chapter
about
temptation

We're all different. Some of us like football. Some of us like basketball. Some of us even like Korfball.* Part of the unique, handmade-ness of every single human being is that our lights get switched on by completely different stuff. Sport is just one example (and plenty of people hate any and every variety of it); you might otherwise be someone who enjoys turn-based role-playing games, or be obsessed with Disney films way into your 20s, or spend most of your free time watching YouTube videos of other people playing board games. And that's not even considering your musical tastes: you might be into hip-hop, classical, indie, emo, hard rock, heavy metal, country, ambient trance, dance, garage, rap, R&B, jazz, funk, techno or third-wave ska.**

*It's a real thing. Look it up.
**As above.

What's more, while you undoubtedly share your tastes with other people (more if you like Taylor Swift, fewer if you like third-wave ska), I can pretty much guarantee that there's no one else on the planet who shares your exact combination of likes and dislikes. Your favourite novel + your best movie + your favourite celebrity x all your dislikes = total uniqueness. You are utterly unlike anyone else who has ever lived, and the journey that you're navigating through life is 100 per cent original too.

Add to that the things that you're good at. There's no one else who's ever lived who has quite your mix of skills and strengths. You may be physically strong or intellectually superior; you could have great emotional intelligence and empathy, or you might be laugh-out-loud funny. Whatever you might think about yourself in your worst moments, there's plenty of stuff you're good at – including the things you don't even know you're good at yet* – and the combination of your strengths is part of what makes you special and different.

I went through the first 30 years of my life thinking I was terrible at every sport ever invented. Then I tried clay-pigeon shooting and turned out to have a knack for it. I'm not entirely proud that the thing I might be best at is firing a gun at things, but in the light of all the other sporting failures, I'll take it. The point is: never stop trying new things. You might be ace at Korfball.

The same is also true of our flaws and foibles. I mean this with great affection, but there's no one else who quite messes up like you (or indeed me). The mistakes we make; our blind spots and weaknesses; these too make up a unique profile. You might be someone who struggles to tell the truth, or who can't seem to stop gossiping; you might be a habitual small-time thief or a long-time porn addict. You'll find some things more difficult than others; some things just don't seem like a problem for you, and some things are a source of guilt and regret every single day.

I could therefore spend the rest of this book going through each of those possible character flaws in turn (if you see them that way), and try to give you some tips on how to improve them. But they're different for each of us, and we feel them more or less intensely, and they combine with other aspects of our character and personality, and mutate into our own unique variant of bad habit or fault.

For that reason, when we come to think about changing and improving some of those things, it makes sense to zoom out and look at the bigger picture. There are some overarching principles which apply to anything we want to improve in, and that's because everything we get wrong comes down fundamentally to the same thing: human imperfection. The highly religious and not very twenty-first-century term for this is 'sin', or even 'the sinful nature'. The Bible uses these words to describe the fact that as well as our natural desire to do good, there's another desire – one that is pulling us in the other direction.

It's all very Star Wars. I don't know if you've seen *The Last Jedi*, but in it one of the central characters – Rey – finds herself in a tug of war between these two forces (or more accurately, two sides to the Force). One is good, positive, hopeful, and brings life; the other is destructive, bleak, evil, and brings death. This same struggle goes on in characters throughout the entire universe of Star Wars films. Some choose the light, others the dark side. The latter always leads to self-destruction in the end, but the path of the former is always much more difficult.

So it is in real life. 'Sin' is easy, and often deciding not to 'sin' is much harder. To achieve the more difficult of the two requires something of us: the power to say no.

The good news is that this power exists, and that not only can we form and develop it under our own steam, but we can ask for a spiritually charged version of it from above. We call this self-control. It's listed a few times in the Bible as a 'fruit of the spirit'; an effect of getting closer to God, which is literally a superhuman ability.* It's something we can ask God to grow and incubate inside us, so that when we sense the pressure of temptation to do something wrong, we're simultaneously aware of the strength to resist it. Self-control is like an increased awareness of the light side of the Force, even as the dark side is beckoning.

*Don't get excited. Other 'fruits' include kindness, gentleness and patience. No matter how close you get to God, you're not going to be flying or commanding thunder and lightning any time soon.

But wait a moment. What exactly is right and wrong? Different value systems, and even different branches of Christianity, will give you different answers. How do you define what's 'sinful'?

On one level, there are some fairly obvious 'sins' which we all agree about. Pretty much everyone you meet is on the same page about murder, for example. It's amazing how quickly that list becomes blurry though: sure, theft is wrong, but is music piracy really stealing? Is cheating on your girlfriend really all that bad if she'll never find out? Are 'white lies' OK if they save someone's feelings from getting hurt?

Your position on all of these things depends on your moral code, and if you draw your morality from the Bible and Jesus, then your list of potential sins is probably pretty long. That's not because God is a killjoy who is looking to trip everyone up into imperfection, but rather because there are an awful lot of ways that selfish human nature expresses itself, and what really seems to bother God is when our selfishness hurts other people. More often than not, we do wrong in the eyes of God because we do wrong to one another.

There are some overarching 'sins' defined by law, but outside of that, your position on what's right and wrong is up for debate. Your moral code – the way you decide these things – is all part of the kind of person you've decided to be. Remember way back in the first chapter, when we talked about your character? As part of forming that, you've naturally already defined a lot of your view on what's right and wrong. If you've decided that you always want to be someone with integrity, who other people can trust, then it follows that you would understand lying and misleading others as a sin. If you value generosity, then meanness with money is bad. If you want to be someone who brings life to others, then selfish behaviour is a problem; if you want to be an encourager, then gossiping and negative talk is wrong.

I imagine some people may choose to define their moral code quite loosely, around what they can get away with. Ultimately though, this kind of selfishness is really unfulfilling, and involves us ignoring our conscience: the brain's natural way of letting us know when our morality has gone a bit wonky. On the contrary, trying to follow Jesus as a role model, and the Bible as a guideline for how to live and treat others, seems to put us much more in line with our inbuilt sense of right and wrong. It's almost as though the same force was behind all of it . . .

Just because our moral code tells us to behave a certain way, however, doesn't mean we do. There's a famous line in the Bible about this: Paul, the guy who helped spread the Christian message around the world like wildfire, says he struggles with the conflict between his aspirations and reality. 'I do not understand what I do,' he writes, in a moment of great existential crisis which he chooses to share in a letter to the church in Rome. 'For what I want to do I do not do, but what I hate I do.' It's like the lyrics to an annoyingly catchy Europop tune. Then he goes on: 'For I do not do the good I want to do, but the evil I do not want to do – this I keep on doing.'*

*You'll find this in Romans 7.15–20. If anyone does manage to set it to a tune worthy of the Eurovision Song Contest, please do get in touch. It could be huge.

I don't know how much you know about Paul, but often he can be quite hard to relate to, like a school teacher who keeps setting really difficult homework tasks. Here though, he really sounds like one of us. We all get what he's saying (once we've got our heads around all the do, do, do's): we know how we want to behave, but we find it hard to do so. Even if you've got a clear and fully formed moral code, it can still be really difficult to live up to it. Self-control is hard.

The temptation to sin doesn't feel like the dark side trying to over-shadow us and take us over. The temptation to sin feels much more like an itch. We suddenly become aware, perhaps because of a moment of opportunity, that part of us wants to deviate from the way we say we want to live. It tickles. It won't leave us alone. We're not overcome by it, but we know the easiest way to get rid of it is just to give in to it.

You know what I'm talking about. It's the last chocolate in the box, left unattended; it's the little lie that will make a whole argument go away. It's sometimes a big thing, like borrowing the car you're not insured for in order to make your day so much easier (until you crash it); it's sometimes small, like clicking *that* link when no one is around. It's a tingling temptation, and fighting it off is a deliberate choice.

Or have you ever given something up, for Lent perhaps, or maybe for sponsorship? No caffeine for 40 days, or no speaking for a whole day? The desire to break that rule is annoying and persistent. We don't have to give in, but for a while we can think of nothing else. It's *itchy*. That's what temptation can often feel like.

I gave up my smartphone for Lent* a few years ago. The first few days were the hardest, and I distinctly remember reaching for my pocket over and over again *just to check*. My phone wasn't there, but it was an impulse – I didn't want to use my phone, but I was instinctively tempted to try. My decision to do something positive was coming into conflict with my instincts, and again, it felt like an itch.

I won't assume that you know what Lent is. It's a Christian trad-ition, based on Jesus' 40-day temptation in the desert (which you can read about in Luke chapter 4). The idea is that you give up something on which you're a little too reliant – like chocolate, caffeine, or in my case, constant social media updates – and therefore make a bit of space in your life for God.

The itches are different for everyone. For some of us, the temptation to drink too much alcohol (or any, if you're under legal age) is an itch; others of us keep gossiping and talking about people behind their backs, even though we wish we didn't. As I said at the beginning of the chapter, we're all unique in both our strengths and our weaknesses; what we're tempted by, and the strength of that itch, is special to us.

Self-control – the power to say no, and as I said, a sort of low-level spiritual superpower – is the best resistance we have to temptation. So as we feel these instinctive desires to break our programming (to 'do what we don't want to do'), engaging our self-control offers our best chance of not giving in.

Right now, stop and think about what the itches are for you. Where do you feel most often, and most heavily, tempted to break your moral code and to go against your decided character?

And then ask yourself: what would practising self-control look like in each case? How would you give yourself the best chance of saying no – of ignoring the itch until it goes away? This shouldn't feel easy – you're on the difficult path of self-improvement now – but it is possible. Itches don't have to be scratched.

Having said that, everyone experiences temptation differently; there seem to be a few 'itches' which are common, and some which come up time and again as I talk to men. That's not to say that women don't also experience temptation in this way, only that it seems that many men do.

Perhaps the most obvious example of this is pornography use.

For a lot of men, the conversation around temptation, and doing what we wish we didn't do, mainly comes down to porn. Surveys of men both inside and outside the Church demonstrate that porn viewing* is widespread, and for many men that leads to a host of negative reactions and connotations ranging from personal guilt to sexual dysfunction. Men – even men with an established moral code – watch porn, and many of them feel bad for doing so. The majority of porn viewing takes place in secret, and most men would never admit to it.

*No one just watches porn. When we say 'viewing', we really mean 'using', and we say using . . . well, you get the picture. Oh, and women watch porn too – just statistically not as much as men do.

We talked a bit about porn in the last chapter, but let's just be clear: porn is vile. It has ridden into the mainstream of our lives on the coat-tails of the digital revolution, and it's now not only freely available but hugely and destructively influential. Porn warps our brains and damages the way we see one another. It sexualizes everyday life and corrupts our expectations of relationships and even casual romantic interactions. It spreads persuasive messages about what sex is for and how you do it, but more importantly it changes our view of how men and women should treat each other. It feeds an idea of sex that is based around total promiscuity and personal gratification, and it usually casts women as second-class citizens, who exist purely to fulfil the perverted desires of men. The people who 'star' in it might be trafficked, or high on drugs, or otherwise coerced and you would never know, and in the end some very rich people are making an awful lot of money out of it. It gets inside our brains and can prevent us from functioning healthily in our relationships and in our sex lives, and it constantly pushes boundaries further and further, as if it's trying to find ever more 'dirty' places to go.

Porn is ugly, and horrible, and destructive . . . but we knew all that already. There's a reason why it's watched in secret, and there's a reason why you feel disappointed or even disgusted with yourself afterwards, and yet still you* look; still you go back for more. Because it itches – not only because of opportunity but because of hormones.

Not necessarily you of course. This might not be your problem at all. If so, feel free to skip this whole section. Or read it so that you can help 'your friend' who does struggle with porn.

Imagine we were reduced to an animal level, where we operated free from morality and just responded to primal instincts. We'd eat when we found food, we'd sleep when we discovered a safe place, and we'd try to mate with anyone we could. Porn pushes our buttons at that animal level. It's like an unattended all-you-can-eat breakfast bar, or a king-size bed covered with pillows. It speaks to our animal instincts and says: there, you can have what you want. It basically treats us like dogs.

But you're not a dog. You're a man, and you've been created with an awesome level of intelligence and inbuilt morality. You have the wisdom to know when to stop taking your plate back to the breakfast buffet, and the presence of mind to stop sleeping after a while. You are also in control of your sexual desires, no matter what your brain might be telling you. Yes, the impulses are strong – and massively enhanced during times of hormonal imbalance – but they're not as strong as you. You can, with God's help, engage your powers of self-control.

You don't have to give in to the little voice in your head that whispers: 'The coast is clear.' You always have a choice: to go out for a walk; to do something else; to make yourself a sandwich. If you're vulnerable when you're left alone, make sure you're not alone; if you tend to look at porn on your phone at night, then leave your phone downstairs. Don't see porn as a guilty secret friend to keep hidden; see it as a sneaky enemy you're going to outwit. And if it gets the better of you today, restart the fight tomorrow. Pornography is far too dangerous to just casually accept – for each of us, and for society as a whole. Some people think that watching porn will teach them to be better lovers; I can guarantee that the opposite is true.

Of course, porn isn't the only itch that seems common to a lot of men. Drinking is another. Again, I'm not suggesting this is a male issue, but often men seem to have a common, culturally warped relationship with alcohol, and it's one that has been passed down for generations. I will have to generalize here and talk about one version of this – the one that I experienced, growing up – if you end up being a cocktail drinker or a wine man, see if some of the general themes translate.

From the age of 16 through to about 21, I probably put more lager into my body than any other substance, certainly including water, possibly even oxygen. I was part of a beer-drinking culture at school, and then at university, where the object of any night out was to see how many pints of the stuff we could consume before we threw up. We would buy glasses and glasses of this fizzy yellow liquid* for ludicrously low amounts of money, as if the bars, clubs and student unions that sold it to us were trying to get us hooked for life.

*It looked pretty much exactly the same on the way out as it did on the way in. This leads me to wonder if the means they really used to keep their prices so low involved a quite horrific bit of plumbing between the bathrooms and the beer cellar.

Most 'good nights out' in those years involved getting so drunk that I could barely remember them the next morning, and came with a free gift – a day of feeling utterly broken afterwards, where it felt like I'd been hit over the head with a baseball bat and then had my stomach punched from within. This feeling usually disappeared just a couple of hours before we went out and did exactly the same thing again.

I don't know how my friends and I got through that period of our lives unscathed – plenty of people tragically don't. The closest we came to disaster was on a holiday aged 19 when a group of us went to the island of Gran Canaria to soak up some sun and bring home hilarious memories. In reality we could have brought home a corpse – one night we went to a party on the other side of the island, and all got so drunk that we didn't realize that one of us had been left behind. He had to undertake an all-night trek across the island, drunk and alone, at one point being zapped by an electrified fence and at another having to escape from the home of a man who turned out not to be as kind as he first appeared. When he finally got back to our resort the next morning, covered in mud, blood and bruises, none of us were laughing. Because although excessive alcohol consumption seems like harmless fun and makes you feel bulletproof, sometimes you're devastatingly reminded that neither of these things is true.

A couple of notable things about that period of my life. First, despite having become a Christian at age 14 and spent my whole teens in a Christian youth group, I somehow managed to suspend any sense of moral compromise in this behaviour. Sure, I was going out and getting drunk, but at least I wasn't doing other 'worse' stuff like sleeping around. Instead of seeing my faith as a relationship with God, where I was genuinely trying to live his way, I was trying not to disappoint my youth leaders too much. And I'd perceived that as long as I didn't commit any sexual sins, I'd get a free pass and a ruffle of the hair on the other stuff.

The second notable thing was that I pretty much *hated* lager. Despite drinking vast quantities on a nightly basis, I never once took a sip and savoured the delicious complex flavours. That's mainly because cheap lager is a bit like smelly alcoholic lemonade, but without the sweet taste. I drank it because of the culture I was in and the image

I projected of myself by drinking it. That all feels vaguely idiotic now, but at the time it must have made some kind of logical sense.

Whatever my reason for drinking, however, and for my ability to somehow carry on doing so even while professing a Christian faith, what seems clear is that my faculties for self-control were completely disengaged during that period. I was either totally unable to say no to the offer of one more drink, or else the thought of doing so simply never crossed my mind.

The Bible doesn't prohibit the drinking of alcohol. Jesus himself was at a wedding early in his adult life, where not only was the bar drunk dry, but he actually miraculously enabled another wine delivery.* What it does say is not to consume so much of it that you lose control. The problem is not the alcohol, but what happens to us as a result; essentially, know your limits and don't get drunk, because when you're drunk, you'll do stuff you regret.

*You're probably familiar with the whole water-into-wine thing in John chapter 2. Jesus did this miracle when the wine had run out, so the guests were already quite inebriated. I'm not suggesting that Jesus wanted to get everyone drunk, but he did obviously prefer the idea of keeping the party going rather than letting it fizzle out.

So once again, this is a matter of self-control. If you identify with some of this – if drinking too much is one of your itches – then think about what you can do to help yourself resist. If you drive, use it as an excuse to stay on the lemonade for a night – your friends will love you for being the designated driver and your bank balance will stay miraculously healthy too. Space out alcoholic drinks with soft ones, or set yourself a limit and stick to it. Just like porn, the promise of alcohol always lies to us. It doesn't make us funnier, or more attractive, and it definitely doesn't make us into a better dancer. What it can do is take away our control, and even our safety.

There can be even darker itches than these. Violence towards others is one, usually a symptom of internal rage that has been left untreated. And violence towards ourselves can be a temptation too. In both cases, developing better self-control might not be quite enough of a solution; we might need to get some help from a doctor or therapist – and there's absolutely no shame in correcting something that's gone wrong in our heads, often through no fault of our own.

We can think of self-harm as a female issue, partly because the media projects this idea. But self-harm isn't just a girl thing, and it doesn't only involve cutting. For guys, self-harm often looks different: like deliberately punching a wall to relieve stress, or taking unreasonably dangerous risks in order to 'feel more alive'. If that's the kind of itch you feel, then you're not crazy, but you shouldn't try to negotiate it alone. Talk to someone you trust, or as a first step visit the excellent website <www.selfharm.co.uk>.

At its most fundamental level, practising self-control is about holding fast to the decisions you've made about yourself. You know all those things we've thought about so far: your character, your purpose, the way you relate to God, looking after your mental and relational health. All those things involve decisions to live your life in a certain way. And of course, anything that's worth doing, usually isn't easy. If you're making decisions which align you less with the prevailing culture, and more with the ideas of Jesus, then you're going to face a certain degree of both internal and external resistance. Your animal nature doesn't want you to elevate yourself, and the world around you wants to sell you a whole bunch of things that will both lighten your wallet and darken your horizon.

So how do we build this muscle called self-control – the bit of you that says no when you're offered a cigarette, or another doughnut, or a one-night stand?

First of all, it helps if we define what we actually stand for. If you're reading this book in a linear order, you're hopefully well on the way to this already. If you know what you think, what your morality is based on, and what kind of man ultimately you want to be, then it's much easier to see where the decisions are. If you know you're someone who stands passionately against people trafficking, you'll simply stop shopping in stores that are known to use slaves. If you've got vague ideas about the ethics of shopping, you probably won't care enough to make a change.

Second, self-control is a spiritually enhanced discipline. That's not to say that people who don't have any kind of faith can't practise self-control: there are numerous examples that prove otherwise. But involving God in our attempts to resist some things and positively practise others, really helps. So, in gritty practice, that means bringing our struggles and our weak points to God in prayer. Now let me just be explicit about this, because it's something I didn't really understand until I'd been a Christian for decades: God cannot be shocked. Don't think too much about it, but he can see everything you're doing anyway. He's not going to be offended if you talk about the bits of your life where you're not quite measuring up. God is not upset by the prayer: 'Help me to resist porn'. God doesn't mind being asked: 'Please help me to stop after a couple of drinks'. If you're taking recreational drugs, he's not angry if you mention it in your conversation with him; in fact, he's absolutely delighted that you're mentioning it at all. Praying about self-control is simply naming those situations where you need more strength to say no, and then asking for that strength.

Third, it's important to be aware of the influence of others on your behaviour. Peer pressure is a massive reason why we slip up in our lifestyle choices, and fall short of the standards we set for ourselves. My first term at university was a complete disaster in this regard. As an extrovert with a massive FOMO problem, I could never say no to one more drink, or to a trip to a club which I knew was going to get me into trouble. I was hugely influenced by my friends, and even more by my desire to feel accepted by them; to feel a sense of belonging. This is not an easy problem to treat, but becoming aware of that unhealthy dependency was key in doing so. If we realize that our friends are leading us into behaviours that don't fit with our moral code, then it might be time either to turn down some invitations, or even to get some new friends.

Finally, self-control is about owning our behaviour, and making difficult decisions as a result. It's something to think about, focus on, and work at. It's the hardest part of truly becoming the man you're made to be: sticking to your principles when almost everything in you wants to do otherwise. You will inevitably slip up, and have to try again; there will be moments in your journey of growing up as a man when you'll wonder whether integrity is beyond you. But work at it, and in the end, as you begin to develop the strength to resist your temptations and your weaknesses, you'll become the kind of man that other men want to be like too.

Think about . . .

As you've read through this chapter, what are the 'itches' that you recognize? What are the things you feel an urge to do, and wish you didn't?

What could you do to help strengthen your self-control 'muscle'?

If you're someone who finds himself looking at porn – and wishing you didn't – what could you practically do to prevent that from happening?

How affected are you by the influence of your friends in some of these areas?

There's one other little thing I want to add before we finish this chapter. Quite a lot of itches are really about the temptation to 'sin' – to step out of alignment with the life we were created to live. But then some itches aren't really about letting anyone else down, God included – some itches are simply our brains trying to take us off into unhealthy and self-destructive territory. We've already talked about how that can result in self-injury and even, tragically, suicide. But there are more subtle versions too, and one of them can be our relationship with food.

There are a lot of stereotypes around food and gender. Girls eat salads and are prone to eating disorders; guys eat meat and are prone to gluttonous overeating. These are accepted cultural norms, and like so many others, we're born into an understanding of them as guys. But although there's a grain of truth in them, they're also largely inaccurate. Plenty of women love steak and there are champion male athletes who are proud of their vegan diet. Similarly, eating disorders aren't only female, and disordered eating doesn't always look like starvation.

If you are suffering from a serious issue with food, it is absolutely OK to ask for help. No doctor will laugh you out of their surgery for confessing to it; it is way more common among men than you would imagine, and they will be delighted to have the chance to put you on the road to recovery. Seriously: please, talk to someone.

If, however, you just have a slightly warped relationship with food, then this is another area where you might need to apply a bit more self-control. Back in Chapter 2 I told you about my own early-teen rotundity, and to be entirely honest, food has been my 'itch' ever since. It started when my dear old grandma, a working-class lady who insisted on spending half her pension on a bag of rich food from a prestigious supermarket for her grandchildren,* started giving me chocolate and crisps on a weekly basis. One afternoon she came with a multi-pack of chocolate bars which my mum hadn't noticed; I sneaked them up into my bedroom and ate all five of them before the sun had set.

I think this was her way of telling the system that she'd beaten it. She never had any money her entire life, but if she shopped there she was able to feel luxurious and wealthy for the four meals she could then afford to eat each week. For non-British readers, there is a UK grocery store where it's almost physically impossible to spend less than £20, even if all you buy is a loaf of bread and some eggs.

After that I started to develop a little paunch, which turned into a bulge, which turned into a belly. Throughout secondary school I retained this look, and also this kind of dysfunctional attitude towards food. Perhaps it was rooted in getting to any given snack before my little brother; perhaps it was just a Labrador-like lack of an off-switch. I saw nice food and I ate it, and I never managed to develop any perspective on how much or how often.

Looking back, I think there were two issues at play. First, I didn't have any resilience or self-control; I was always a kid who would give in easily, and I couldn't seem to push myself to delay gratification. If I saw chocolate, I ate chocolate, and I never developed any resistance to that. Second though, I think I learned to see food as the ultimate reward; something I 'deserved' whenever I'd worked hard or completed a task, like finishing my exams, playing a sport or walking to the fridge. In fact, I should have learned to reward myself in other ways.

As a result of overeating I got fat, and as a cruel result of that, I got bullied.* Now I am not justifying that, or blaming myself – bullying is horrible and never the victim's fault. But I still wish I'd had a healthier relationship with food in my teens – and to be entirely honest, still today. This is my itch, and the temptation to scratch it continues into my forties.

Ah yes, I promised to tell you the words to my old theme song. I only do this on the basis that I am trusting you never to sing this to me if we ever meet. It went to the tune of an old football chant: 'He's short, he's round, he bounces on the ground: Fatty Saunders, Fatty Saunders.'

If this resonates with you, then I think all those ideas about self-control apply here too. Avoiding temptation, making good decisions, and perhaps also being aware of how friends can influence our eating choices are all important. Above all though, this is yet another area which God cares about, and wants to help us with. God loves it when we talk to him about the real stuff – even if the real stuff is our inability not to order the supersize milkshake.

7.
Banter: a chapter about friendship

Who is your best friend? If you were in a tricky situation and contacting your family to get you out of it wasn't an option, whom would you call? Who is the person your age you like, respect, and in some ways want to be a bit like, more than any other? Who is the friend whom you know you can always rely on, who rarely lets you down, and whom you think you'll probably still know and love 20 years from now (it's not a trick question; you don't have to answer: 'Jesus')? Who is the friend whose personal suffering – should the unthinkable happen – would devastate you too? Got that person's face in your mind?

Now here's another question: do they know? Do they actually understand that this is how you feel about them? I don't mean, have they probably picked this up by osmosis? I mean, have you told them?

I would guess that in 90 per cent of cases, the answer to that question would be no. And allow me – having been so painfully 'right on' for the first six chapters of this book – to make a sweeping gender-based stereotype at this point: if I asked that same question to a group of women, the overwhelming answer would be yes.

Generally speaking, this is another area where men tend to behave in a certain way, not because their testicles dictate that they must do so,* but because these are the rules of the world we've grown up in. We don't tell friends – and particularly other men – how we feel about them because of a fear of how we'll be perceived by them and others. If you ask most men how they know their best friend likes them, it's highly unlikely the answer will be 'because he told me'.

Imagine that. I think I've just invented the world's least family-friendly supervillain: Nutman. He attacks whole cities because of a tiny megalomaniac who lives inside his testes. Surely Hollywood will be knocking my door down within seconds. Anyway, there is a bit of a hormonal aspect to all this, so I suppose there is a physiological aspect to the problem; I'm just suggesting the cultural part is stronger.

One morning when I was 13, my friend Tim was hit by a bus. I wasn't with him at the time; a flurry of gossip spread around the school just as it was about to start for the day, and it reached me as I was on my way into the building. Instinctively I ran to where he and I usually got off the bus and crossed the road together. I'm not entirely sure what I was hoping to do when I got there, but logic is not your first calling point at moments like that. I arrived just as the ambulance drove away; there was nothing I could do.

It was a long time ago, but I still remember the pain in my chest (not from the running, cheeky), and the sense of utter panic. More than that though, I distinctly remember a feeling of regret. Tim was my best friend; we'd gone through nine years of school together and we were usually inseparable in the holidays too. And what went through my head was this: if Tim is dead, he'll never know what a great guy I thought he was.

Relax: Tim wasn't dead. He broke a couple of bones and was back in school the following week. When he did return, however, I made sure to sit him down, look him in the eyes and tell him how much he meant to me. I told him he was my best friend, and that I wouldn't have known what to do if he'd been hurt more seriously. It was, from memory, an excruciating exchange. We'd never talked like this before (and come to think of it we never talked like this again); it just didn't make any sense in the context of our friendship.

There have been a few other occasions in my life when friends have been very sick or otherwise in danger, and I've journeyed through a similar chain of events with them. I've felt regret at leaving things unsaid, and I've taken the opportunity afterwards to tell the guy that I care about him. In pretty much every case it's felt incredibly awkward, but I've pushed through. Yet it still feels strange for both of us, because this *isn't what guys do*.

From my experience, not just of living my own life but of observing many young people over the years, boys and men are also fairly bad at encouraging one another. We don't generally say complimentary things about one another's clothing or hair; we don't congratulate one another on achievements – large or small. We don't tend to glory in one another's successes.

In contrast, the thing that men seem to be very, very good at in our friendships is what British people call 'banter'.* This is an interesting word, because although it sounds friendly and jokey, it's also fairly meaningless out of context, and can mean different things to different people. What it really seems to be is a cover word for mutual unkindness between apparent friends. In many friendships, banter seems to be the primary basis for interaction. We have banter with our friends as a way of avoiding any more serious interaction; we trade hilarious insults as a way of entertaining ourselves and engaging in a never-ending game of passive one-upmanship. In fact, for our closest friends, we often reserve the edgiest and most outrageous jokes, as if you can only say truly horrible things to people whom you trust won't punch you for it.

*I shared this word the other day with a group of young people I help to lead; they looked at me blankly. Apparently, the word has now

eroded and regressed into the form 'bants', or even '#bantz'. I despair
of the growing illiteracy of the younger generations sometimes, really
I do. Not you though. You're reading a book; look at you.

By this strange logic, the way we therefore know who our best friends are is by thinking about who is most likely to put us down, tease us, or bring up our weaknesses in public. Our greatest friends are probably the guys who often behave as if they're our most sworn enemies. Now, of course I'm exaggerating to make a point, but there's more than a kernel of truth there.

When you add this to the 'Tim' problem outlined above, you start to see quite an issue emerge. We make fun of our friends, but we never encourage them. We make them aware that we know exactly where their weak points are, but we seldom take the time to tell them that we value them, instead assuming that this is implied by our presence in their lives. In essence, we never actually tell our friends: 'I like you.'

I sat recently with two 12-year-old lads who are – as far as I can perceive their relationship – great friends. Yet during a series of conversations which was actually about friendship, all they did was say horrible things to and about each other. They smiled throughout; they laughed as each tried to outdo the other. They were having fun, both of them. But I couldn't help wondering: how does either of them know that the other guy doesn't secretly hate his guts?

Here's a stark contrast: a woman said to me recently that she knew she was loved by her friends, and that this had become a source of security for her when someone else let her down. She knew instantly who she could call in a crisis; she knew exactly who would have her back. This felt really positive and healthy. My fear is that for many men, the reality is very different. We *think* our friends like us, but that's based on assumptions, rather than knowledge and evidence that we could pin down.

I want to suggest that this is not what healthy friendship looks like – in men or women, or indeed between the sexes. That's not to say that we shouldn't do any of the things mentioned above, but just that they shouldn't be the dominant principles – the basis even – of our friendships.

I have this one friend, Robert, who seems to be quite good at the alternative. It may help that he's American, and therefore much less cynical and naturally gnarled up than me and my British mates. He's six-and-a-bit feet tall, handsome, helpful, and one of the nicest people I know.

Robert is not afraid of a little bit of banter. He'll make jokes when my football team loses (especially when it loses to his), and he might make fun of me for wearing something unfashionable. But largely the things that I hear him say to me sound like 'well done' or 'I loved that thing you said', or even 'I appreciate our friendship'. And here's what's interesting: by doing that he normalizes male-to-male encouragement; he makes it OK for us to say nice things to each other, and he inspires me to follow his example.*

*As I say, it may not be a coincidence that Robert is an American. Generally speaking, those guys seem much more comfortable with encouraging and building up their friends than us Brits. In our culture, we're so cynical that our first reaction to a compliment is deep suspicion.

In some senses this (slightly generalized) problem with male friendship is easy to diagnose, and also fairly straightforward to treat. We make too much fun of one another, and we don't support and encourage one another nearly as much as we should. We therefore need to shift the balance so we can feel fairly confident about those relationships.

Of course, it's not quite that simple. As much as we shouldn't behave in this way, there are strong reasons why we do. And until we address those reasons, it's not a simple case of changing behaviour.

For a start, banter is culturally ingrained in us as the way men treat one another. Increasingly ours is a culture that prizes wisecracks and one-liners,* and that's often displayed in media depictions of male friendship. For example, take the scene in *Avengers: Infinity War* where Tony Stark and Dr Strange meet for the first time. Despite the fact that they're trying to combat the looming threat of universal annihilation, they are prepared to waste quite a long segment of the film poking fun at each other with biting daggers of sarcasm. Tony derogatorily calls Strange 'The Wizard'; in response Strange is witheringly sharp about Tony's shortcomings. And these guys are on the same side!

There's a whole social networking site based around this idea. If you're under the age of 25, don't worry; it's called Twitter, and your parents probably have accounts.

The long-running sitcom *Friends** offers a slightly healthier version of the same phenomenon, where characters do occasionally take a break from all the put-downs and take time to talk about their feelings, but in the context of a show that ran for 200+ episodes and averages a joke every 10–15 seconds, this is still overwhelmed by the banter. Joey and Chandler, held up as a great example of positive male friendship since the early 1990s, actually make fun of each other an extraordinary amount. And while you might argue that this is kind of the point of a situation comedy, there's also no denying the influence of what they have now subtly role-modelled to several generations of viewers: men mainly do banter.

Yes, I know Friends *is about a hundred years old, but in a 2019 survey it was voted the most popular show among teenagers and young adults. Don't think I'm not down with the kids; I just did an* Avengers: Infinity War *reference.*

Another thing which drives banter between men is insecurity. This isn't always the reason why men pick away at one another, but it's often present. We feel uncertain about our own value, and so we subtly attempt to pull others down with us. It's pretty strange that we choose to use friendship as the vehicle for this kind of dysfunction, but it makes a weird kind of sense. Our friends are the people around whom we feel comfortable enough to share our insecurities, but in a banter culture, the way we share them is through humour instead of honesty. So believe it or not, your friend who is teasing you about your test score, or your relationship, or your video-game skills, is probably doing so partly because they feel nervous about their own achievements in exactly the same areas.

Sometimes friendship gets competitive, and this is often as unhealthy as it sounds. Tied up with our insecurity, we get sucked into comparison with one another, and comparison can lead to competition. Because our friends are the people we know best, we naturally score ourselves against them. There are some areas of life where this happens almost automatically: exam results for instance, or sporting contests, or even applying for the same job, and it's hard not to at least notice our own positions or results in comparison to theirs. If we're not careful though, we can carry that same approach into a whole bunch of other situations. We can compete with our friends to be more popular, or more 'known'; we can compete to look hotter or be better-dressed than them, or even to be more successful in attracting partners. These are not the hallmarks of healthy friendship, but again they become legitimized by a jokey culture of banter.

We'll need to be mature here for a moment, but I want to suggest that good friendship isn't characterized by how sharp the banter is between us, but by how well we love one another.

That's a pretty big statement, I know. We don't tend to think about male friendship in terms of love, partly because of centuries of homophobia in the heart of our culture. But we should – platonic love between guys is a thing to be celebrated, and what's more, it's something we clearly see in the life of Jesus.

Remember the story of Lazarus, the friend of Jesus who died while he was away? When Jesus arrived to resurrect him, he was overwhelmed with emotion. But while the Bible only describes that emotional reaction in two words, it gives us a little bit more from the people who observed the situation. Seeing his tears, the onlookers exclaim: 'See how he loved him!' (John 11.36). They are so struck by the depth and passion of Jesus' response that they can find no other word for it than love. It's hard to imagine Jesus' friendship with Lazarus as being mainly banter-based.* Rather that it was characterized by two men caring deeply for each other.

Although someone should *imagine that; it sounds like the basis for a great first-century sitcom:* Jez & Laz: Just for the Bants.

Jesus had a lot of other friends. He travelled around with 12 of them for three years, and within that group he had some even closer associates. His friendship with Peter was strong enough to withstand betrayal – Peter denied knowing Jesus once it came to the crucifixion, yet received forgiveness from his friend – and another disciple is described as 'the disciple whom Jesus loved' (John 13.23). Again, there's no suggestion of anything romantic here; it's just that Jesus was a guy who truly loved his friends.

So what could that kind of love look like in our lives? Fundamentally, it's about putting our friends' needs above our own. Jesus talks about this idea quite a lot: at one point he says that 'Anyone who wants to be first must be the very last, and the servant of all'

(Mark 9.35). What he means is that if you want to get top marks in his eyes, then you need to put everyone else's needs and wishes ahead of your own.

That probably sounds a bit crazy. Why on earth would we want to become the least of all people? Why would we want to prefer everyone else's needs, hopes, dreams and agendas over our own? What happens to all the things we want?

Follow the logic though. In Jesus' version of friendship, you put all your friends' needs ahead of your own. But if they're all doing the same thing, then the only person in your entire friendship group who isn't putting you first . . . is you. Do you see how brilliant that is?

In this version of friendship, an issue like competition disappears – unless of course you're competing to out-prefer one another. And insecurity simply melts away; you know that your friends have got your back because they constantly remind you of the fact. You might make jokes, but you also might take a moment to consider one another's feelings before you launch into an ever-nastier exchange of put-downs.

The thing is that this kind of idealistic view of friendship applies a bit of pressure to our relationships. Not all of our friends are going to want to subscribe to this way of interacting with one another, and as painful as this might be, that's because they're not really our good friends. In fact, changing the script of friendship from banter to love is a great way of finding out who your real friends are.

A good friend is one who cares what happens to you. He's* someone who wants you to do well, rather than not quite as well as him. He's someone who would be devastated if you were hit by a bus, but also makes you aware that you're important to him while you're still alive and free from tyre-marks.

Yes, I know that men and women can be friends; this chapter is about male friendship because of the peculiarities of that. I fully appreciate that great friendship can and should exist across the gender divides; it's just that it's usually more functional and doesn't require all this advice.

A good friend is someone who loves you. And that means that you can and should love your friends too. And let me just make this just a tiny bit weirder: a great blueprint for that kind of love is found in a Bible passage which usually gets read at weddings. Actually, although it's been co-opted for that purpose, it's not about romantic love at all: it's about the love of God, which all of us should try to imitate. 1 Corinthians 13 is perhaps the most famous piece of writing about love ever written. So take romance out of your thinking, and ask yourself: isn't this a pretty great vision for friendship?

Love is patient, love is kind. It does not envy, it does not boast, it is not proud. It does not dishonour others, it is not self-seeking, it is not easily angered, it keeps no record of wrongs. Love does not delight in evil but rejoices with the truth. It always protects, always trusts, always hopes, always perseveres. Love never fails. (1 Corinthians 13.4–8)

For a start, the author – Paul – says that as human beings we're essentially empty without love. Then he lists all these different attributes of love: things which signify our loving nature. I think it reads like a little manifesto for how we could treat one another:

Patient: I want to be the kind of friend who sticks by other people, who doesn't lose my temper when they slightly let me down. I will try to remain calm.

117

Kind: Essentially, I seek to be a good guy, who values other people and wants good things to happen to them. As much as I'm able, I'll play a part in making those good things happen.

Not jealous: I refuse to give in to the instinct for competition. If my friends do well, I will share in their glories, rather than feeling cynical or bitter about them.

Not boastful or proud: When things go well for me, I won't rub it in my friends' faces. Instead I'll invite them to party with me. I might even pay for the cake.

Honouring of others: I won't betray my friends, including in the way I talk about them. I will not get drawn into gossiping or talking negatively about my friends; in fact, I'll stick up for them.

Unselfish: I will try to put my friends first.

Forgiving: I will accept my friends' apologies, and I will not keep dragging up old arguments.

Protective: If my friends need me, I will be there; I will even put my body on the line for them.

Trusting: I will choose to believe my friends, and always believe the best in them.

Persevering: Even when things are tough, I will be there for my friends.

Doesn't that feel like a bigger, better, more revolutionary vision for friendship? Instead of basing our relationships in banter, wouldn't they feel so much more secure on this kind of footing? And think even bigger: what if whole friendship groups, or even whole communities of men, started to treat one another on the basis of this set of principles? How different would the world start to feel?

I believe that this is the kind of friendship we were made for. Not for teasing and insecurity, but for deep, lifelong loving relationships. And of course, this can only start with us. For a culture to change, someone needs to go first; so how about starting to treat your friends this way, following the example of the man who once said: 'Greater love has no one than this, that one lay down his life for his friends' (John 15.13, niv84)?

Think about . . .

Do you recognize a culture of banter in your friendships and groups? How do you feel about it?

How big an issue is comparison for you? Where do you notice it most?

Do you compete with your friends? In what ways?

How do you feel about trying to love your friends?

Which of the aspects of platonic love listed in 1 Corinthians 13 would you find it easiest and most difficult to apply to your friendships?

*

8.
Same:
a chapter
about
technology

It's probably an obvious thing to say, but the world has changed a fair bit since I was a boy. In fact, it's changed more during that time – let's charitably say the past 25 years or so – than it has during any point in history since the Industrial Revolution. The arrival of the Internet, the accompanying advances in microtechnology and the combination of the two in the smartphone has rebooted our culture to such a degree that some aspects of it have changed beyond all recognition.

Other things are still pretty much the same – to the point that some sci-fi films made in the 1980s and 1990s are now starting to look a little foolish in their predictions. We don't yet have flying cars, or self-piloting aircraft, and we still cook food instead of ingesting little three-course-meal tablets. The sky thankfully hasn't been scorched by nuclear war, aliens haven't invaded as far as we know, and very few people have a home robot.

Other things have perhaps changed a little more, to the point that their 1995 equivalents are now becoming museum pieces. We no longer jog around with large cassette players* clipped to our shorts, nor do we own cameras that can take a maximum of 24 photos (photos that you're not allowed to look at or check until you've paid for them to be printed). We don't have to carefully plan our evenings around the start times of our favourite, never-repeated TV shows, and nobody has a dedicated phone in their car.

The cassette Walkman is a little hard to explain if you've never seen one. Just imagine a large plastic box, inside which you would slide another bulky piece of plastic, the size of a phone, which contained a single album. Now imagine this was the year's must-have Christmas present, and that you'd make your parents pay extra for versions that said meaningless things like 'Bass Boost' on the side. I promise you, that button did nothing.

In some regards though, the world has changed completely. It was conceivable 25 years ago that we'd have found a way to make cameras digital or personal entertainment devices smaller. We imagined that graphics would get better and technology would get smarter. But the Internet we never saw coming. The idea that the entirety of wisdom and knowledge collected through all human history would be hosted in a single virtual place, and then made fully searchable in milliseconds via a tiny portable device – that really would have seemed like fanciful sci-fi set in the very distant future. Or the idea that we'd all be instantly connected to one another, to everyone we grew up with, to long-lost family members on the other side of the world, through constantly updated networks; or that normal people would make millions of dollars by broadcasting make-up tutorials from their bedroom; or that you'd be able to play a photo-realistic video game with 100 random strangers all around the world. It would all seem too much – and yet it's reality. And with the rate of change being as fast as it currently is, even this paragraph will feel nostalgic in five years' time. So if you're reading this in 2024, my apologies for being so far off the pace.

Depending on your age, you may well be classed as a digital native, which means that you have grown up during this Communications Revolution. Opinions differ on how old you can really be and still get away with being classified in this way, but 35 (at time of writing) is the absolute peak.* If you were born after about 1995, you certainly count, and therefore almost certainly know more about this topic than I do. I was born in 1978, back when you could get away with making puppet-based television shows, and the best video game in the world was *Space Invaders*.

Can I just say – since I haven't said it before – that if anyone over the age of 35 is reading this book, you are and have always been most welcome. I think a lot of this stuff translates across the generations, and most of the time I'm just preaching to myself anyway. Also, I hope you've noticed that I've tried to put a few jokes and references in just for you, rather like the gags they put in to make the Shrek *films bearable for parents.*

If you *are* a digital native, then you almost certainly understand the technology, and the terminology that correctly describes it, better than most people in the older generations. It doesn't necessarily follow, however, that you naturally make the wisest choices about *how* to use it. This takes wisdom, a few personal decisions and – given that you've read this far, I'll assume you're OK with it – maybe a little bit of advice too.

My wife and I have four children. The eldest was born in 2005, the youngest in 2013, and they are all very much digital natives. As I write this very sentence, Naomi (11) is watching a TV show on a tablet,* while Joel (13) is playing an online game on the PlayStation. Samuel (8) loves to catch up on episodes of *Match of the Day* on demand, while Zachary (5) once tried to interact with a printed photograph by pinching it, then looked confused as to why it hadn't zoomed in. If they were allowed to, they'd probably use games, phones and screens much more than they do. That's because these things are all designed to be highly entertaining. As their parents though, we put some rules in place about what technology they're allowed to interact with, and how much. We do that because we love them, and because we can see a bigger picture, beyond the lure of all those pixels.

*Now there's a phrase that wouldn't have made much sense in 1995.

I am not your dad (unless you're reading this Joel, in which case, don't panic). I'm not here to tell you what you can and can't do. But in this chapter, I do want to make a few suggestions about how you might want to navigate the complicated and fast-changing digital world. It's up to you what you do with this advice.

The way you decide to behave online, or in other engagements with technology, is another element of the man you're choosing to be. You might think you can separate yourself into different versions – online and offline, or even a variety of flavours of you spread across different social networks, games and platforms – but, ultimately, you're still always you. So if you truly want to decide to live by a moral code, to shape your character and to approach life with a sense of purpose, then these things have to span every digital version of you as well as the real thing.

Our brains can trick us into thinking that's not true. Incognito browsing which doesn't leave (as much of) a digital footprint, avatars or screennames which hide our true identities, game skins and private accounts: they all give us a misguided sense that this stuff doesn't count because our names and faces are hidden. But they're not hidden from us. We still know that it was us writing that snarky comment under a pseudonym; we know which websites we visited in private browsing mode. Social media trolls, who use specially created accounts to send hateful messages to people they often don't know in real life, still have to look themselves in the bathroom mirror before they go to bed after an evening of making lives miserable. You can't hide from your own conscience behind an avatar, and if you do, you're creating a nasty crack in your own integrity. This book is all about taking responsibility for who we are, and the scope of that continues into how we act through technology.

The person you are online is still the same person you are offline. If you behave differently, then it's no different from your suddenly deviating from your usual conduct in real life. So imagine that – having decided you were going to be kind – you walked into a branch of McDonald's and started shouting abusive comments at other customers, preying particularly on the weakest people in the restaurant. Or say that you were a rational and sensible person, but on a bus with a stranger you suddenly descended into a loud argument in which you swore several times and got personal in order to win your point. If you did stuff like this, you'd probably get some very strange looks, but more importantly, you'd be failing pretty badly at being the authentic you. So why is it any different if you do the same things in a virtual space?

Technology can give us what feels like a free pass. At the more harmless end of the spectrum, we can shoot people in video games when we wouldn't dream of doing so in real life. But it gets complicated pretty quickly. If a friend offered you a ride on a stolen bike, you'd probably decline. But if he sent you the link to a stream that would allow you to watch a pay-per-view sporting event for free, might you click it?

The trouble is that we don't stop so readily to engage our character, and particularly our sense of integrity, when we're online. That's why people write appalling comments on videos and pictures, or watch content they don't legally own, or access content that they shouldn't. None of these are activities that these same people would engage in offline.

One of the saddest examples of this is the rise of so-called cyber-bullying. Emboldened by the distance of the screen, young people – perhaps even those who would never normally engage in real-life bullying – target others in their school or community with a range of digitally enabled techniques. They might create a fake Instagram profile which shares vicious comments about the person tagged in each image; they might create secret WhatsApp groups which an individual knows about, but to which they are not invited, and then use them to spread unkindness about that person. There is a wide range of ingenious and unpleasant ways to bully others through social media and technology, and perhaps the most disturbing thing – aside from the difficulty often experienced in trying to catch the perpetrators – is that they draw in co-conspirators* who would never normally behave in such a way.

*If you are tempted to join in with the bullying of another person via digital means, stop, and if possible, do what you can to bring it to an end. On multiple occasions, these kinds of incidents have ended in the victim's suicide. That's how serious this is.

The first and most important piece of advice, then, is to make sure that the online you is still you. There shouldn't be a fault line between the person you present online and the person that people meet offline. You shouldn't be the sort of charming young man in real life that people would gladly introduce to their mother, and a monster once you get behind a computer. And if you are, then it would suggest there are some things to sort out in your character; you can't just put it on pause because you're logged into a faceless social media account.

The next thing to consider is how much time you're going to spend on screens. My hunch is that most of us are a bit like a Labrador dog in this regard. Labradors are famous for not having an off-switch; if you place a small plate of food in front of them, they will gladly eat it, and then walk away looking a bit sad. If, however, you place an enormous plate of food there, they'll clear that just as happily. And if you were to accidentally leave the entire several-kilogramme bag of dog food unattended in the open, an untrained Labrador may well munch her way through the entire thing in one sitting. So it is with screens. Some of us seem to have inbuilt off-switches; we tire of technology after a while, step away from the screens and do something else instead. Some of us, however, are Labradors; we'll play as much PlayStation as we're allowed, while keeping an eye on phone notifications, and possibly also a third screen showing clips from YouTube. Now, just because a Labrador *can* eat her way through an entire sack of food, it doesn't follow that she *should*, or that this is good for her. In the same way, it's possible to live most of our lives through our phones, games systems and computers, but that doesn't mean it's a good idea.

Screens are brilliant in lots of ways. But they're also incredibly addictive, and are designed to entice us to use them more and more. So if possible, it's a really good idea to make some decisions about how much we want to use them, while we're not actually using them. And without wanting to be too prescriptive, you might want to set yourself* some aspirationally low limits.

One of the great innovations of the past couple of years has been the emergence of 'screen time' apps, including Apple's own inbuilt system on their phones, which allow us to either limit or monitor the amount of time we spend using certain aspects of our smartphones and other tech. Even if you don't strictly bar yourself after a certain time limit, I'd encourage you to check this sort of thing occasionally to see if your perception of your amount of screen use is in line with reality.

'Screens' is also far too broad a term. In a minute I'm going to be a bit more specific about a few different types of technology, and what a healthy approach to each might look like. But here's one overarching thought: screens and digital spaces are an accompaniment to, not a replacement for, real-world interactions. If you realize that you're spending much more time engaging with people online than face-to-face, you may have got the balance wrong. By all means play sports games, but also get some exercise. Message and update your friends, but also meet up with them in person. Phones and other screens can trick us into thinking we're having lots of human interaction, when we're really only trading bits of data.

Now, I get that for some of us this is easier than for others. I am a raging extrovert,* and therefore the greatest source of energy in my life comes from spending time face-to-face with other people. For many people, this kind of contact only brings life when it involves a few close trusted friends, and for still others, it's just easier if everything happens virtually.

*Get to know if you're an extrovert or an introvert, if you don't already; it'll change your life. My wife, a classic introvert, describes my need to constantly spend time with other people as being 'like a sickness'. I'm the sort of person who tries to befriend shop assistants and make conversation with random strangers in airports; you're probably inclined to agree with Mrs Saunders.

There are also some people for whom online interaction offers a refuge from the cruelty and complexity of the real world. If you suffer from anxiety – social or otherwise – or you experience bullying or massive shyness, then the technological advances of the past decade or so have thrown open the doors of opportunity for you to socialize more widely and profoundly. But even if that's you, I'd implore you not to lose touch completely with relationships in the real world. Even if they're costly, they're important.

So, to tackle a few specifics:

Social media – normally accessed through smartphones – is a fantastic innovation. It means we can stay in touch with a much larger group of people than ever before; it enables us to stay on top of break-ing news and follow developing stories; it even gives us direct access to celebrities. Mostly, it's great for keeping track of the lives of the people we care about, but it has a dark side. As much as we might try to deny it, we make ourselves incredibly vulnerable when we post on social media. We might try hard not to care, but we can quickly become obsessed with tracking the response – or lack of it – to what we've posted. If our notifications start pinging with kind comments and 'likes', we're quickly delighted. If there's only silence, we can start to feel a mild sense of panic about our own declining popularity.

There's actually a scientific reason for this. Dopamine is your brain's inbuilt reward system, a neurotransmitter that's released whenever you achieve something, like completing a work task or an essay, or going for a run. It can also become artificially stimulated by nicotine and other drugs. Dopamine is also released by your brain when you spot a 'like' or a positive comment on a social media interaction. This explains not only why you feel good when you get this little burst of online affirmation, but also why people become addicted to social-media-based appreciation. They are literally feeding off the same brain response that is triggered by cocaine. The trouble is that the need for this little buzz begins to drive the way we operate online, to the point that we can stop posting for the sake of sharing news and start posting in order to harvest affirmation. You see, the highs from Dopamine are great, but the lows can be devastating. If you're experiencing dopamine withdrawal because suddenly no one is liking your Instagram posts, it can actually feel a little bit like grief.

The way to counteract this is to make sure you take regular breaks from social media, and downgrade – or at least own – its importance in your life. As I write this, I'm about six weeks into a total break from all social media. I know I'll be back at some point, but I realized that it was starting to have far too much of an impact on my life and my sense of well-being. I would spend evenings frustrated by things I'd read; I'd trip into arguments with total strangers and lose hours to conversations that would never be resolved. But more than any of that, I realized that my brain was craving dopamine from these interactions and leading me to spend more of my free time online than was healthy. As a result, my offline, real-world friendships were suffering, and I needed to do something about it. I've had more conversations with my great friend Matt, for example, since I stopped using Twitter and Facebook* than I did in the whole of last year – and he just moved 150 miles away.

Yes, I know, I'm still very much rooted in old-man social media. Your grandparents can follow me on Twitter @martinsaunders. I also have an Instagram account, but can't really work out what the buttons do.

Taking this break has rebalanced my priorities quite a lot, but it's also been a helpful reminder that online and offline friendships are not the same. When we meet face-to-face, we communicate and relate in all sorts of ways: words, facial expressions, gestures – and more than that, we give one another our undivided attention. When we communicate online, we only use a fraction of all those faculties. Social media is great, but it is a poor substitute for real socialization.

Smartphones are also pretty incredible.* It's no exaggeration to say that the computing power that we now walk around with in our pockets is greater than that which all of NASA used to put people on the moon. We can play complex games, take hugely detailed photographs, listen to most of the songs ever recorded, watch an encyclopaedic collection of TV, read books and access all of the aforementioned human knowledge with just a few swipes of our fingers on a tiny device. Now, most of us just use them to send funny cat pictures to one another, but the potential is awesome.

*Don't get me wrong in this chapter. I love technology. I could bore you for hours with stories of how my dad used to bring home the latest innovations when I was a child. In fact, I'll probably do that in the next footnote.

The trouble is that smartphones, like and partly due to social media, turn us into notification addicts. Have you ever felt the urge to grab and check the phone in your pocket, and then realized it's not actually there? That's because our muscle memory is so used to performing that action, we instinctively reach for it, even when it's charging. But most of the time it isn't charging, it's in our pocket, constantly being pulled out and checked again, just in case there is some small piece of breaking news, or an SMS message, or a new funny cat picture to look at.

Smartphones also become screens in another sense – barriers between us and the real world. Have you ever stood at a live music concert and observed what happens in the big songs? My wife and I went to see Ed Sheeran at Wembley Stadium last year; and for most of the gig it seemed like around a quarter of the crowd were filming everything on their phones. I can guarantee you two things: first, none of those people ever watched any of that footage back, and second, exactly the same thing would have been posted to video sharing sites by hundreds of other people standing at slightly different vantage points. So all of those people watched the best bit of an £80-a-ticket gig through the screens of their mobile phones . . . you could wonder what the point was of them being there at all.

Again, the best way to break the hold that the smartphone has over you is to take breaks from it. Leave it at home occasionally; turn it off when you go out for dinner (instead of Instagramming your food, because frankly, no one cares). This is a real demonstration of strength and self-control. You'll be amazed at how liberating this is, and perhaps also slightly scared by how often you reach for it.

Video games were pretty much my favourite thing growing up, and honestly, looking back you wouldn't believe the rubbish that I used to play on my home computer.* We would play text-based adventures, which had absolutely no graphics at all, or blocky, eight-colour platform games that are almost impossible to imagine in their simplicity and ugliness. Technological advancement was slow and steady as I grew up; I'll never forget walking into Barkman Computers in Kingston-upon-Thames and hearing the first game that managed to make use of the speech chip in the Sega Megadrive – *Sonic the Hedgehog*. It was only one word, and it sounded like it was being spoken by a robot underneath a muffly blanket, but it felt like the future had arrived.

My dad worked for ICL, which was a computer company. He'd often bring home their latest machines, which even then looked like equipment from a retro sci-fi film. Fortunately, he was also interested in what the rest of the market was doing, so we'd also have some of the latest systems and games in the house. When I say 'latest systems and games', remember that this was the mid 1980s, and if you saw these things now, you'd assume they'd been coded by a pre-schooler.

Then during the late 1990s and early 2000s, there was a gear change. Suddenly games started to look and sound better and better, and over the decade that followed they were on a speedy journey towards movie-style visuals and immersive realism. No longer were you bashing the buttons of a joystick to make a little character jump on to a ledge and collect a gem; now you were looking through the eyes of a paratrooper on the inside of a mission behind enemy lines in the Second World War, or sitting behind the wheel of an exact replica of a Formula One car.

Graphics and gameplay continue to improve year-on-year, and now the video game industry is bigger in terms of revenue than Hollywood. I imagine if I was a teenage boy today, I would be begging my parents to let me spend every waking hour on my PlayStation or Xbox. But just because I'd want to do that, it doesn't mean that would be good for me to do so.

Again, this comes down to self-discipline. We have to realize that if we spend all our time playing games, then other things are suffering. There is only so much time in the day, and if we choose to use hours of it on immersive missions in the Star Wars universe, then what happens to things like exercise, sleep and social time? As with social media, meeting up with your friends in a game of *Call of Duty* is definitely a social experience, but it's not a replacement for real-world friendship. So by all means be a gamer, but make sure you're in charge of your games console, not the other way around; being able to decide to switch off and do something else is a demonstration of strength.

Finally, the **Internet** really has changed everything, and is the force which enables all the other things above. There are lots of things on there that are helpful and healthy, and lots of things that are not. We've already talked about some of that. The overriding principle* is not to allow the web browser to trick you into thinking that none of this counts. Downloading stuff that you haven't paid for, or watching illegal streams, counts. Peeking inquisitively at explicit images counts. Trolling people counts. Encouraging people to hurt themselves or share inappropriate photos counts. All of it is the same; your character is tested and displayed just as much online as offline.

*Apart from 'try not to look at porn'.

The Internet wasn't around when Jesus walked the earth, and I think subliminally we can imagine that he's not really interested in it.

When we do that, we forget that he's outside of time; that he knew about social media a million years before Snapchat was invented. And what he cares about is us: how we live out our lives through screens as much as in real life, and how potentially we can hurt and diminish ourselves or others.

In the 1990s there was a weird craze in the Church which still has some devotees today. It was called What Would Jesus Do? and involved wearing a wristband embroidered with the initials 'WWJD'. The idea was that you'd look at your wristband as you were about to sleep with someone, loot a store or murder an enemy, and then think – hang on, would Jesus behave like this? It was designed as a character-development tool: a way of reminding yourself that you were trying to live in a way that imitated Jesus.

As cheesy as it sounds, I think it's actually quite a healthy filter for our relationship with technology. Even if you're not personally a Jesus devotee, hopefully we can all agree that he excelled at being wise, and would imagine he'd do technology better than most of us. It's not a bad thing to ask yourself, any time you feel tempted by a little bit of moral compromise. Here's a couple of things that Jesus said, which might have an implication for how we act online:

> Simply let your 'Yes' be 'Yes', and your 'No', 'No'.
> (Matthew 5.37, niv84)

> Whoever can be trusted with very little can also be trusted with much, and whoever is dishonest with very little will also be dishonest with much.
> (Luke 16.10)

Jesus urges people to act with integrity – to be honest and trustworthy – while the greatest temptation of the digital world is to act with a little dishonesty, about who we are and what our boundaries and principles might be. So engage with technology – play games, check your phone, take a picture of your lunch and share it all over the world – just never allow these to be the places where you lose sight of who you really are. On and offline, you are the same man.

Think about . . .

What do you observe about your online behaviour? Are there ways you behave differently online from offline?

Does your behaviour or persona change and shift between different kinds of technology? Are you different or the same on various social networks and games?

What kinds of boundaries do you think would be healthy for you around:

* social media?
* your smartphone?
* video games?
* the Internet?

How do you find yourself tempted to let your moral code flex a bit online? What can you do to stop that?

9.
Better:
a chapter
about
women

On the very first morning that I started writing this book, I saw something which very clearly reminded me of one of the main reasons for writing it in the first place. I was sitting in my favourite coffee shop, squished into a corner like some sort of hibernating rodent, planning out the list of chapters I thought would constitute a coherent journey* through modern masculinity. A woman walked into the shop – 25 years old or so – wearing jeans and a t-shirt. No one could possibly argue that she was provocatively dressed, but she was pretty and made-up, and there's no other way to put this: she had large breasts.

   *That's right. Believe it or not, there was a plan behind all of this. Eleven chapters, woven together cleverly so that by the end you'd be able to step confidently into your full potential as a man. How's it going so far?

From the second she walked into the room, men were noticing her. Some were pretending not to, looking up at her subtly at guarded intervals. Others were much more blatant – two student-age guys shared a joke at her expense; a table full of workmen put down their coffees and simply stared. As I looked around the packed coffee shop, almost every man in there was voyeuristically keeping an eye on her, as if she might be about to ask one of them at random for a date, or strip naked in the middle of the queue. She actually just wanted a coffee. She didn't seem to enjoy the attention, and she got out quickly.

For me this provided a stark reminder that as a culture we're not nearly as progressive as we might think, or claim to be. Despite all the campaigning, all the rebalancing we've seen in the media, business and elsewhere; despite the fact that we all know the *right thing to say*, there are still some very deep-seated attitudes and prejudices that men hold towards women. Girl walks into room in anything other than a giant poncho, men stare. Same as it ever was.

But not all men, right? Not all men treat women like that; we don't all stare at them when they walk into a room in tight-fitting clothes; some of us aren't even attracted to them.* Not all men treat women without the basic dignity and respect that they deserve as our fellow human beings. Well yes, but . . .

If you're gay, you don't automatically get a free pass on this. Stereotypically you might be a bit better at empowering and equalizing women, but you're still part of the wider issue, as I'll explain.

In recent years, a hashtagged phenomenon called #MeToo has brought some ugly revelations to the surface of our culture. After several high-profile men in the Hollywood movie industry were unmasked as serial abusers of women (and in some cases, men too), women around the world, in every stratum of life, began to reveal their own awful experiences at the hands of men. Using social media as a platform to raise awareness of the size and scale of the issue, normal women everywhere talked about how they'd been subject to sexualized violence, rape and other abuse. Suddenly this was no longer faceless victims 'over there' somewhere, but real people in our communities, girls and women that we knew personally.

At the time of the original wave of #MeToo revelations, I was doing a bit of work as a freelance journalist.* As a result, women started to get in touch with me, not because I'm somehow above all this, but because I was someone who might be able to share or amplify their stories. One by one I'd read emails and messages from old friends and acquaintances, and occasionally from women I knew really well.

I know this is quite a serious section, but I should probably point out that I've never been regarded as a serious or hard-hitting journalist, or even a particularly good one. Mainly I did a line of Christian culture comedy clickbait lists, which were about as broad-appeal as they sound.

Some of them wanted to talk about how they'd been poorly treated because of their gender: as the punchline of sexualized jokes, or receiving unwanted comments about their appearance. Some had felt genuinely harassed, or even been promised promotions or other rewards in exchange for sex. And then there was another set of stories which just seemed to get more and more horrifying.

I was aware that some of these women had been victims of sexual violence. But in all cases I had no idea of the scale, the details, the lasting effects or the fact that they'd simply had to bury the past without ever seeing a perpetrator brought to justice. One friend was attacked on a tube escalator in rush hour. Another received an unwanted back massage at work which quickly moved on to her breasts. Another was threatened with assault by three men in a train carriage while commuters looked the other way. Another was raped by her older brother. Another was sexually assaulted by a group of friends at a party. Yet another was painfully attacked by a youth leader who was supposed to be teaching her to be more like Jesus. I could go on, and tragically, on. This wasn't a collection of stories from a group of survivors, these were simply drawn from women I knew. For a while it felt as if every woman I knew had experienced something like this.

But, of course, as I said earlier, 'not all men'. Not every man is a sex offender, and not every man is violent. Not every man treats women with contempt, or a sense of sexual entitlement. This much is true.

Yet even if you haven't harassed or attacked a woman – and I pray you haven't – you've almost certainly played some passive part in their oppression. If you've ever looked the other way as a woman was humiliated for what she was wearing, if you've ever been part of a locker-room conversation objectifying girls; if you've ever watched porn, which has the most twisted gender ethics of all and is responsible for the increased sexualization of women everywhere – then you're part of the problem. As bitter a pill as it might be to swallow, #MeToo was about you too.

(Ugh, hang on a minute. This is all suddenly very serious. Eight chapters of gentle life advice, and suddenly we're talking about objectification and passive oppression? Well forgive me for lulling you into a false sense of security, but the trouble with toxic masculinity – the stereotypical, ill-fitting yet strangely still-popular version of what it looks like to be a man – is that toxicity burns; and women are too often the victim.)

Every man is born into a system where for thousands of years, people like us have been in charge. Our society is built on a long legacy of what's called patriarchy (literally: where the fathers rule); men have owned the power and the money for thousands of years right around the world. Women have played a subservient role to men throughout history, being seen and indeed defined as second-class citizens. In many countries, including the UK, they couldn't even vote until the last century. And while huge progress towards gender equality has been made, today's women still feel the shockwaves of those millennia of oppression. In fact, it's more than that; the system might appear to have changed dramatically, but underneath the surface, this patriarchy is still alive and well. The difference in pay between the genders is still vast; the real power in boardrooms throughout the business and finance worlds is still held by men. And as I write, the most powerful man on earth,* elected by one of the apparently most progressive countries, is widely accused of both sexual abuse and harassment. An assertion from the man in the street that things have changed, and that 'the feminists have taken over', is about as in touch with reality as those people who think the moon landing was filmed in a secret TV studio.

This book has been refreshingly free of even a whiff of Trump – which in itself is a joke only British readers will understand. If you're an American reader, however, and perhaps even one growing up in a Trump-supporting household, I apologize for any offence caused by my suggestion that he's bad news. But you should know, just in case you don't, that the rest of the world literally cannot believe that he was elected as your President.

So as part of that system – even if we don't feel like particularly willing participants – we are part of the wider context where sexual violence between men and women is a far-too-common occurrence. This is shameful, and until we accept that we're part of the problem, and feel a bit of reflected shame on behalf of our sex, perhaps we'll never truly see things change. Because if we acknowledge that we're all part of the problem, maybe it also follows that we could form part of the solution.

As we've discussed, all of this starts from a young age. Building on a rich heritage of sexism, we believe boys are sportier, smarter,* more natural leaders, more independent; even more naturally destined to reach 'the top'. In short, boys are raised – by the whole world, not by one individual source – to believe that they're *better* than girls. That men are *better* than women.

Sure, we all know that girls are sometimes academically stronger than boys, but when it comes to a broader version of 'smart' – to include cunning, streetwise guile and general common sense – guys tend to believe themselves to be superior. That's why so many stereotypes exist around driving, home improvement and humour.

142

Sexual violence isn't the only problem that patriarchy brings, but it is one of the clearest possible indicators that the balance of gender equality is seriously out of whack. And that imbalance will only change when men accept that they are not *better* than women. And that starts with you, and with me.

When we think about what kind of men we want to be in the world, this is one of the most fundamental and far-reaching decisions we can make. Let's break years of programming, and centuries of influence, and not only stand against inequality in some sort of abstract, intellectual way, but practically demonstrate in the way we live our lives that we do not believe ourselves to be better. Let's intentionally be people who not only recognize all the prejudice of history, but are wise enough to spot its influence, and brave enough to carve out a different future.

We can decide to be offended or defensive about #MeToo; we can claim that not all men are part of this and argue that we'd never do anything to hurt a woman. *Or* we can allow ourselves to be shocked, saddened and sobered by it – and by all the inequality of history – and then be moved to action and change; to step up and be a part of a worldwide movement of men who agree together not to repeat the sins of their forefathers.

This isn't just *the right thing to say*. It's part of becoming the man you're made to be – not to diminish women who, like you, are made in the image of God, but to be an ally as they break out of a man-made system of oppression, and get the chance to live up to their fullest potential alongside you. Classically men are cast as rescuers, but that's not what this is – women aren't all princesses, and this isn't another tower to break them out of. Rather, this is about breaking ourselves out of a system that casts us all as yet another generation of clueless tower-builders. By default, we will just repeat the problem; we have to decide that things are going to be different.

If you're going to take Christianity as the basis for your code and character, and follow Jesus as your role model, then this stuff is really non-negotiable. Throughout the four main books of the Bible in which we read about his life on earth, Jesus treats women with equality and respect, even in the midst of a culture that didn't. It's hard to get our heads around the culture of the year AD 30, but back then, women were so far from equality with men that the very idea would have seemed laughable. Women had fewer rights, less of a voice and less of a role – perhaps less than we can even imagine. Yet Jesus befriends them, gives them instrumental roles in his mission, and most importantly, talks with them face-to-face.*

I realize that this doesn't sound like a big deal, but he would probably have been pretty unique as a leader in his lifetime, in the way that he treated and included women. Imitating Jesus today doesn't mean that it's good of us even to talk to women's faces; following his example now means being equally radical about gender in comparison to the rest of culture.

Earlier on we looked at how Jesus talked at a well with a woman who had been left utterly ashamed by a combination of her character and her culture. If a man in that same time and place had behaved similarly, and made morally questionable choices, it's unlikely that he would have been left as a social outcast. In a culture where sexual sin was usually cast as a female fault, this woman couldn't even go out to draw water at a time of day when she might have bumped into other people. By treating her with respect and reinvesting her with a bit of dignity, Jesus refuses to participate in the broken view of sex and gender in his society. Fast-forward 2,000 years and we see the echoes of this story in the way male and female promiscuity is viewed. In men, it's still seen as strangely heroic to sleep around; in women it's seen as unpleasant – there are accompanying derogatory labels which prove as much. In our culture, I imagine Jesus wouldn't praise promiscuity, nor would he cast it as unforgivably shameful.

Rather he'd call people to something better – the fulfilment of sacrificial, monogamous relationships or of singleness – and make no distinction in that message between men and women.

In a male-dominated world, it's been an inconvenience for centuries that the first person to see Jesus' resurrection – arguably the most important eye-witness moment in all of history – was a woman. Mary, one of Jesus' close friends and disciples,* is standing weeping outside his tomb, when he appears to her. She thinks he's a gardener at first, but then realizes it's him, right in front of her, back from the dead. Now, even though there are male disciples in and around his empty tomb, Jesus chooses to appear to a woman. And just in case we might think this is a coincidence, and nothing to do with gender, Jesus tells her: 'Go to my brothers [the male disciples] and tell them.' Even in that culture, at that time, he puts the most important news ever shared in the mouth of a woman. This is the clearest possible indication Jesus could give to us – at the very turning point of history – that he's not playing the *men are better* game. He makes no distinction, and nor should we as his followers.

No, she wasn't one of the Twelve. But a lot of Bible scholars believe that there were plenty of women around Jesus the whole time, but because of all the patriarchy, only the men's names got written down, except in situations where it couldn't be avoided. Maybe that's why Jesus appeared to a woman first (in John chapter 20): so that no one could airbrush her out of history. Even so, for centuries powerful men have sought to smear her with the unsubstantiated claim that she was a prostitute – perhaps in an attempt to weaken her influence.

It's one thing to agree intellectually with the idea that men aren't better than women. It's quite another to put that into practice. There are so many subtle ways that gender imbalance has wormed its way into our culture; disarming all those bombs means having our eyes wide open to every form of them.

For instance . . . when women and girls wear short skirts, there is a culturally accepted assumption that they are behaving suggestively – or as some might put it, 'asking for it'. In fact, they may just enjoy fashion, and be making the most of their physical features, not for anyone else's enjoyment, but for their own pleasure. It's horrific to think how judges and juries have shown leniency to rapists because their victims were 'provocatively dressed'.

For instance . . . language really matters. Saying that someone is 'being a big girl', or 'throwing like a girl', or 'parking like a woman' should never be an insult.

For instance . . . when we hear or see sexism in action, it's easy to turn away and pretend we haven't. It's incredibly hard to challenge the attitudes of others, especially in front of our friends or people who might laugh at or criticize us for doing so. But unless we do, nothing changes.

In all of this, we have to be consistent – not simply saying female-affirming things when we know we're being overheard. What that really means is making a deep-down, heartfelt resolution to be different. I've often known men who are incredibly supportive of women when in the public eye, but make revealingly sexist jokes when the coast is clear. This is just another kind of betrayal. We have to take this stuff to heart, to resolve to change – to do better.

I don't know about you, but I want to sit in a coffee shop where a woman can walk in without the fear that half the men in there are going to stare at her chest. I want to live in a society where people are paid what they deserve to earn, regardless of whether they happen to have a penis. I want my sons and my daughter to grow up in a world where men don't believe – on the surface or on some deep level – that they're better than women. Instead, I want them to be part of a world that doesn't even see that as a contest any more. You and I can play a huge part in making that world real.

Think about . . .

What are some of the subtle prejudices you still hold about gender?

Do you agree that as a man you automatically become a part of the gender injustice problem? Why do you think you think that?

How do you accidentally treat girls or women differently when you shouldn't?

What one thing could you do to make things easier or better for the women around you?

What one thing could you change about your attitude towards women?

10.
Everything:
a chapter
about
materialism

When I was 12 years old, I robbed my mother.

Alright, that's putting it a *little* strongly. Don't picture me as a young thug, holding my mum at gunpoint while she clears out the family accounts. I saw her purse unattended one day, and I saw an opportunity. Rustling through it with my heart pounding, I fished out two shiny one-pound coins, and slipped them into the pocket of my *Teenage Mutant Ninja Turtles** hoodie. I had a pang of conscience but I ignored it; this money was going to get me the thing I desired most in the world, and the end justified the means.

   I don't know if you'll find this interesting, but when I was a kid, they launched the kung-fu kicking turtles in the UK under the more family-friendly name Teenage Mutant Hero Turtles. Apparently 'ninja' had the wrong connotations for a kids' TV show. They seemed to think 'mutant' was perfectly acceptable though.

Closing up the bag and hollering upstairs that I was going out, I pressed on immediately with the task of spending my ill-gotten gains. I headed straight to the newsagent at the top of my street, and went shamelessly inside. Because, dear reader, I was collecting World Cup Italia '90 football stickers, and my collection was about to get a lot bigger.

A packet of six stickers cost 20p back then – not a huge amount for the thing I coveted most in the world. The stickers usually bore the faces of players from the 24 teams due to compete in the football World Cup that summer, although occasionally you might get lucky, and find a shiny national team logo, or even the most prized sticker of them all: the golden World Cup itself. Mostly though, they were just pictures of guys named things like Igor Belanov (USSR), whom I had never heard of, never saw play, and only remember because he was the gateway drug; the first sticker I ever got.

It seems ridiculous now, but at the time I was completely consumed by the quest to complete my sticker album that spring before the tournament began in June. I would stand in the rain with my friends at school, frantically swapping duplicates because you weren't allowed them in the classroom; I would spend every bit of pocket money I got on another few packets. And as I've already confessed, my obsession even drove me to do the worst thing I'd ever done: steal from my own parents.

I took my ten dirty packets of stickers home, and raced upstairs to my bedroom. I ripped open each one like a man possessed, sorted the stickers into 'got' and 'need' piles, and then began carefully attaching them to the relevant pages of the album. After ten or so minutes I was done; my bedroom floor littered with cast-off sticker backings from a reward I hadn't earned. And then I realized what I'd done, and I felt awful.

It struck me that I had become so obsessed with getting what I wanted, I had completely lost sight of whether it was right for me to get it or not. Now, with the prize that I had obsessively pursued safely in my grasp, I was struck by the emptiness of it all. And then, a few minutes later, the inevitable consequences of my sin arrived. Somehow* my mum had worked out the details of my brilliant heist. She banged on my bedroom door and told me I was grounded for two weeks. It was a fair cop.

At the age of 12, I had imagined myself to be a brilliant and un-detectable thief. I hadn't, however, factored in my mother's ability to remember how much money she'd had in her purse, and to deduce that the ten empty sticker packets in my bedroom bin might somehow be connected to its sudden disappearance. To be fair, she reads a lot of detective novels.

I'm glad to say that I felt guilty before I got caught, not because. And while I realize that many people commit far worse crimes before they reach adulthood, I think this fairly ridiculous example is a helpful metaphor for something much bigger. There are lots of ways in which we all run after the things we want to get in life, without stopping to ask if we actually *should* get them, or whether it's right to get them in that way.

What does success look like to the average person today? Some people (better people than me) might give a great and aspirational answer to that question involving making a difference, changing the world for the better and treating others well. Generally speaking though, the broadly accepted answer is mainly defined by 'achieving' in life and work, and the natural indicator of that is personal wealth; the accumulation of money and 'stuff'. If you ask an average group of guys – and I have – what they would most want to get out of life, there will be some common answers: a well-paid job, a big house, cool holidays, a nice car. That's the dream, even if they don't person-ally think they have much chance of achieving it.

There are some other repeating answers too: good friends, a great partner, and perhaps also children. These are excellent hopes, and perhaps not all that surprising given that we were made for relation-ships, not solitude. Yet what's interesting is that when I've talked to young men about those kinds of dreams, they become distracted by the first set. A beautiful wife would be great, goes the logic, but you're more likely to get one if you have a fast car and lots of money.* If you want to have kids, then you'd better make sure you can afford to give them the very best start in life. Even: you're more likely to be popular if you've got a bit of money to flash around.

Just to disprove this theory, I have only one of the three. I also drive a banged-up Volkswagen Touran and work for a Christian youth charity, so I'll let you figure it out.

There's some logic in all of these ideas of course, but they're also all horribly flawed. Money doesn't buy you love, or happiness, as we all know. So why do we pursue it, and all the other stuff that it can bring you, so relentlessly?

The biggest reason is that we confuse the things that we want with the things we need. But they're different. If you're the sort of person who doesn't mind writing in books, grab a biro; otherwise grab a piece of paper. Now, try to make two lists: the things that you absolutely, definitely need in order to thrive as a human being, and then the things that – even if you feel like you desperately need them – you only actually *want*. As you think about this, some items will be easy to categorize (oxygen feels like a bit of a non-negotiable), but others are a little more complicated. Do you really *need* a smartphone, for instance? Would your life be massively diminished without one?

I've started you off with a couple of examples, but feel free to continue (or cross out mine if you don't want a sports car):

Need	Want
Air	Games console
Water	Sports car

Now look at your two lists (or if you're the sort of person who doesn't do these kinds of exercises, think about what you would have written on them). What do you notice?

For a start, there are probably a fair number of things on your 'need' list. We are complex beings, and we have a variety of needs, including friendship, education, medical care and more. There's probably also a long list of wants – and don't feel bad about that. We naturally desire lots of stuff, and given that we're all living in a culture that is constantly trying to sell it to us in a whole variety of ways, that's hardly surprising.

On that need list though, I imagine you've naturally also written the most important things in your life: friends, family, reciprocal love. These things aren't just important, they're also completely priceless. You can't pay someone to fall in love with you, or even to truly care for you as a friend. These are the aspects of life that we know we truly need, and they're also the things that we desire most deeply. If you talk to someone who is at the end of their life,* they'll probably never tell you they wish they'd had a bigger house or a better car, but in most cases if they do have regrets, it'll be that they should have spent more time focusing on things that were ultimately free to obtain.

*An end-of-life-care nurse named Bronnie Ware wrote a book called The Top Five Regrets of the Dying. Cheery, right? The people she spoke to wished they'd stayed in touch with their friends, and that they hadn't worked too hard. One of the greatest gifts of having older people around is that they can help us not to make the same mistakes they made. So, don't work too hard; see friends instead. Simple.

Some of the distinctions you made between your two lists might have been painful (especially if you put your phone on the 'want' list). There are some things which feel so connected to our happiness – a favourite video game or beloved series of books or comics for example – that it's hard to imagine life being happy and fulfilling without them. And imagine now if I told you that you'd never have any of the things on your want list, ever again. That would be hard, right?

The other thing that you might notice from this exercise is that there's sometimes a difference between the amount of something that we want, and the amount we actually need. Go-large fast-food meals are a great example of this. You never *need* large fries, but you almost always want them. Afterwards, when you feel slightly sick from the large milkshake, you wish you'd stuck with the regular portion. You may have written something similar on your lists; you *need* a means of transport, but you'd *love* a great car. Or you need enough money to pay your bills, buy food and afford shelter, but you'd *love* to have so much money that you never had to worry about running out. Quite often our dreams are about having an abundant amount of the things we need.

Many of the world's problems are rooted in exactly this issue: wanting more of its resources than the share we actually need. Millions and millions of people live in abject poverty, but there are individual people who could afford to feed most of them from their own personal wealth. If those guys (and yes, they're always guys) clubbed together, they could probably solve the problem. Yet they don't, because losing the entirety of their wealth would somehow count as a failure. So when we buy into a system which says that success looks like wealth accumulation, we're becoming part of the same broken world view that keeps people in awful conditions, with nothing to eat, all around the world.

Jesus says something interesting about all this. It's one of a few of his sayings which seem to contain such universal wisdom that they have passed into common usage among non-religious people. He's talking to his disciples about what success looks like, and then he asks a rhetorical question: 'What good is it for someone to gain the whole world, yet forfeit their soul?' (Mark 8.36). Or in other words: you can think you have everything, but in reality you've got nothing. You can spend your whole life pursuing money, wealth, fame and power, and then get to the end of it with nothing in the bank.

It's quite an interesting saying to consider, when you're trying to work out what sort of person you want to be. Another, more positive way of putting it might be: don't focus on gaining stuff, but instead, do what makes your soul flourish. We have a choice about where we focus our energies, and we can decide not to buy into the accumulation culture if we want to. We could not only recognize the things that are most important, but actively invest ourselves in them. You could give your life to making money and getting stuff, or you could give your life to something more profound.

Jesus reserved some of his harshest words for the wealthy. Rich men came to see him, to ask if there was a way for them to join his movement and retain their status and position, and he sent them away distressed. He even told one that 'It is easier for a camel to go through the eye of a needle than for someone who is rich to enter the kingdom of God' (Matthew 19.24).* Now, it's important to note that he wasn't saying that people who had lots of money and stuff couldn't join him, but if they were going to, they'd have to agree to a pretty dramatic change of focus.

*He wasn't quite serious, and he's not suggesting anyone tries to liquidize a camel. Bible boffins think he was making a clever joke about getting through the tiny gate in the city which people called 'the eye of the needle gate'. You'd certainly have to get off your camel to get through it, and that would have been very embarrassing and undignified for the rich because their animal was a symbol of their wealth.

What Jesus is getting at in both these sayings is that when we spend our time going after the things we want, we can actually lose out on the things that we need. If we dedicate our lives to the relentless pursuit of stuff, we'll almost certainly end up making sacrifices involving friends, relationships and family. If we throw ourselves head first into the world's version of success, we risk missing out on a better, happier life.

I know men who have found themselves caught up in what they call the 'golden handcuffs' of a high-powered job. They earn huge amounts in the financial sector, but in order to do so they have to work long hours, often stretching into weekends too. They travel the world on business, but often only see the insides of airports and hotels. Meanwhile their children grow up in huge homes, attending fantastically expensive and well-resourced schools. Yet these children never see their fathers, and when they do – on a ski trip or at a poolside in the Caribbean – they know that at any second a vital email could wrench them apart again. Often these men describe a desire to change course, but once you've bought into a lifestyle that expensive, it's hard to see how that's possible. It's not difficult to see why the rich man walked away from Jesus so disappointed.

It is far easier to make a decision in the earlier part of your life that you're not going to embrace such a lifestyle, than it is to decide to leave it later on. So the question is: do you really want to aim for a life that has such an inbuilt lack of balance? Is money really the commodity that you want to have most of?

There's nothing wrong with money of course. Even the Bible doesn't say that money is evil – in a verse that often gets misquoted, it only says that the *love* of money is the root of all kinds of bad stuff. What's wrong is fixating on and overprioritizing money, because usually if you're gaining lots of it, someone somewhere is missing out or getting hurt as a result.

For most of us though, money is simply the gateway to the things we want. If we desire a big bank balance, it's only because that big bank balance will help us to pay for material possessions. Deep down we believe that better cars, bigger houses, more technology, more Instagrammable holidays – all of them made possible by earning or borrowing money – will make us happy. Yet while all of those things are enjoyable in the moment, they're not what induce long-term, meaningful happiness.

The actor Jim Carrey was once the biggest and highest-paid star in Hollywood. His films, such as *Ace Ventura: Pet Detective* and *The Mask*, were among the biggest-grossing of the 1990s, and Carrey was handsomely rewarded. He enjoyed the absolute pinnacle of the American dream: 'making it' in the movies. And he was a household name all over the world. Financially speaking, he was free to never work again by his early 30s. Yet later in his life he reflected on that incredible success by tweeting: 'I hope everybody could get rich and famous and will have everything they ever dreamed of, so they will know that it's not the answer.' And a few years earlier, a novelist named Jack Higgins who enjoyed similar success and saw many of his books adapted into films, was asked by a reporter if there was anything he wished he'd known when he was younger. Higgins replied: 'I wish somebody would have told me that when you get to the top, there's nothing there.'

These two men have known both the victory of achieving the ultimate aim of fame and fortune, and the despair of realizing that it doesn't bring the fulfilment that it promises. So if money, stuff and even fame aren't the answer, how can you choose a better way?

When I asked a group of teenagers about success recently, I partly did so in order to provide myself with ammunition for this chapter.

I expected them to list off all the 'earthly' things that might classically signify a successful person: money, possessions, a big house and so on. Frustratingly for my point, however, a brilliant 16-year-old girl named Lucy was first to reply, and suggested that success meant making a positive difference in the world. Now, you never want the first person to shout out the correct answer, but I think she was right. Leaving the world a better place than you found it would be unquestionably more satisfying than dying in an enormous mansion surrounded by classic cars. And I think that's the flip side of Jesus' famous words to the rich. His little joke about camels and needles isn't intended as a bar on the door to heaven, but an invitation to shrug off all the ultimately meaningless stuff that we weigh ourselves down with, and pass through that gate into a better way of living: the kingdom of God.

Jesus died on the cross in order to open up the way between humanity and God. Sometimes though, we only really talk about the individualistic side of that: that Jesus died for me personally, and you personally, and for your friend Trevor.* He did do that, he absolutely did. His death makes it possible for you to have a personal, individual relationship with God, which means that when you pray, he listens; that he's interested in the minute detail of your life; that he has missions and plans for you, and he offers you life that genuinely lasts for ever. All of this is good and true (and exciting).

*Apologies if you or any of your friends are called Trevor. I didn't pick on it because it's a funny name. It's a strong, manly name meaning 'Slayer of Dragons', and you should be proud of it. Anyway, what do I know? I'm called Martin.

That's not the whole story though. Jesus died for each of us, but he also died for *all* of us. He died for communities, and people groups, and nations, and ultimately the whole world. His death and resurrection are like a trumpet blast which announces the arrival of a better world – a world which is good news for all those people. Have you seen that bit in *The Lord of the Rings: The Two Towers* when Gandalf appears with the huge army of reinforcements who come to overwhelm the evil orc hordes? It's a bit like that: Jesus appears on the horizon of a dark world, and announces its salvation.

The world today is a pretty dark place. There's huge inequality and massive injustice. Racism and sexism still bubble close to the surface of our culture, and selfishness is everywhere. Jesus' death, and the different kind of kingdom that it announces, has something profound to say to all of that. The Bible tells us that Jesus' kingdom – of justice, love and freedom – is slowly eclipsing the kingdom of darkness, of which we see so much evidence around us. In the last book of the Bible, Revelation, we read a promise that God 'will wipe every tear from their eyes. There will be no more death or mourning or crying or pain, for the old order of things has passed away' (Revelation 21.4). This is a picture of how things will be when Jesus returns to earth, and completes the switchover between the existing kingdom and the one that's still emerging. And however dark the world might be right now, we can be certain that this is eventually where we'll end up.

So that means we have a choice to make: which kingdom do we want to be a part of? Do we want to buy into a system of 'stuff', where we win by accumulating more than the average person? Do we want to sign up for a corrupt, and ultimately unfulfilling journey towards a full bank balance and an empty heart? Or would we rather sign up to be a part of Jesus' advancing system of justice, compassion and love?

I imagine you're aware of the 'right' and 'wrong' answers to that question. But in truth, your allegiance isn't demonstrated in a single decision, but in a constant, ongoing string of them. Each day we either step closer towards the kingdom of God, or trip backwards into the murk of selfishness.

Part of this is about our general direction of travel: what we're aiming for in life, and what kind of success we're feeling ambitious for. A lot of the time though, it's simply about how we choose to live each day. A choice between slightly more expensive, fairly traded chocolate or coffee, and cheaper but potentially exploitative alternatives is one example. A decision to put money in a charity collecting-tin instead of buying something we don't really need could be another. Choosing to take money from my mum's purse in order to buy football stickers was certainly a step in the wrong direction.

Hopefully as we reach the closing pages of this book, you're feeling intrigued by the radical call of God; the crazy idea that you might have been made for more than just consuming stuff until you die. In some ways though, this is the most radical decision of all: to reject wealth accumulation as the mark of success and the key to your future happiness.

In one of his stories,* Jesus describes a farmer who keeps harvesting crops and finding that he has far more than he needs. Instead of giving the extra away or working to feed the hungry around him, he just starts building a bigger barn. Sound familiar?

It's called the parable of the rich fool – just in case you were in any doubt – and it's found in Luke 12.13–21.

The man is delighted with his plan, but promptly drops dead that night. It leads Jesus to comment: 'Watch out! Be on your guard against all kinds of greed; life does not exist in an abundance of possessions.' It's Jesus' way of warning us that storing up wealth just doesn't pay off how we might imagine. Life does not exist in an abundance of possessions. So don't choose the possessions – choose life.

Think about . . .

What does success look like for you – in the long term?

What kinds of decisions might you need to make in order to pursue this success? How might those decisions have an impact on others?

How do you respond to Jack Higgins's suggestion that 'when you get to the top, there's nothing there'?

What do you think of the idea that Jesus came to save broken systems and communities and our entire way of living, not just because of our personal sins?

What can you do practically today to step a little further towards God's kingdom, and a little further away from the dream of selfish accumulation?

11.
Pursue:
a chapter
about
adventure

I spent nearly five years trying seriously to make it as a Hollywood screenwriter. It was a slightly hair-brained idea, but no matter how much my close friends tried to remind me that the odds of achieving that goal were slightly worse than those for getting repeatedly struck by lightning, I couldn't shake the desire to try.

It started about 15 years ago, when my friend Stuart suggested that I might* be good enough. He'd read a draft screenplay that I'd sent him – an as-I-now-think-about-it-unfilmable caper about an obese detective in the 1980s – and called me to say that he thought I might have a chance of getting some paid writing work, if I applied myself to learning the craft.

*I don't blame Stuart. To be fair to him, he only said 'might'. He has subsequently gone on to become fabulously successful, and now directs medium-budget Hollywood movies like The Shack.

For the next year or so I dedicated myself to that end. I read about writing, practised, and then wrote page after page of mostly mediocre filmscript. And do you know what? It went quite well. At the end of the year I'd managed to win myself representation in Los Angeles, and after four years of writing, meetings and various flights across the Atlantic, I was sitting in the home of a major Hollywood star, surrounded by actors and movie industry people at a read-through of a film I'd written. I had a script in my hand with the logo of a major talent agency and my name on the front, and it looked like the dream was really going to become a reality.

And then it didn't.

But this isn't a story about glorious failure, even though I guess that's an inevitable part of it. I'm not even sad about it. This is a story about five years of adventure, and how God was with me every step of the way.

Over the course of those five years, I went to amazing places, saw incredible things and met extraordinary people. I went to the wrap party for the original *Transformers* movie with a whole load of A-list stars and a huge unattended buffet,* I walked around the lots of various studios, and missed meeting Steven Spielberg by 30 seconds. I stood next to one leading man in a bathroom, and accidentally flirted with another at a dinner party. I took meetings with people who could make my wildest dreams come true, and I got to talk about creative ideas with some of the most innovative and brilliant people on earth.

There's a whole story here that I'm still not ready to commit to print. But suffice to say it involves 37 mini slider burgers, a major Hollywood pin-up and a unisex toilet. Ask me in person.

All through this crazy journey, I was aware of God's presence alongside me. It was the adventure of a lifetime, and even though I did much of it several thousand miles from home and the people I loved, I never felt even slightly alone.

Here's what it looked like: when I was writing, I would start each day by praying – asking God for his help. When I was travelling, I made sure that there were times when I did nothing, where I simply allowed myself to become aware of his presence nearby.* Before meetings, I spent time reading old prayers and parts of the Bible. And while I can't prove that God was with me, somehow actively involved in this process, I saw some pretty incredible doors open. Because honestly, I wasn't a good enough writer to have done all that on my own. You even have the evidence of this.

This might sound crazy, I know. I distinctly remember being in the waiting room of a car rental place at LAX airport, just before the most important visit of my life, and it was like everything went into slow motion. God's presence was as real to me as this book is in your hand. It was like an invisible fog, which of course makes no sense at all.

What happened in this phase of my life was that my purpose clicked into gear. I had worked out who I was, and what I was on the earth to do, and I pursued it. I set off on an adventure not with a sense of blind ambition, but of tenacious devotion to living my life to its fullest potential.

That last phrase isn't mine, by the way. It comes from Jesus, who says in John 10.10: 'I have come that they may have life, and have it to the full.' That is genuinely his desire for all of us: that we should be able to squeeze every last drop of richness, flavour and meaning out of our lives. My experience over those five years – and in plenty of other moments since – was exactly that; it was hard work, and scary at times, but I felt as though there wasn't a single bit left that wasn't being pushed and developed. I grew fast, I saw plenty of small dreams come true, and very nearly achieved my biggest ones.* All throughout, it felt like an adventure, where I never knew what was coming around the next corner. And God not only made it possible, he made it better.

I haven't given up, by the way. I'm still writing romcoms. Sorry if you were hoping they'd be explosion-filled action epics, but you probably know me better than that by now.

As you reach the end of this book, hopefully you've spent a fair amount of time reflecting on your character – who you are – and how it's developing, which is who you want to become. You've perhaps also thought about this idea of purpose: what it is you're here to do with your one wild life. My hope is that I've made a good case for using Jesus as the role model for how you process those big questions, and that as you've thought about the different dimensions of what it is to be a man, you've seen how his way of living and being makes good sense.

So perhaps you now find yourself in the place I did just before the story above began. You know you're not the finished article, but you have plenty of intent. You've resolved to be one of the good guys, and now you're ready to get started on your heroic journey.

If so, then great. The world needs more men like you, in every area and sphere of influence. At a time when good leadership seems to be in such short supply, we need men like you in politics – wading into the murk of local and national government because you genuinely want to make the world a better place, not because you're driven by money.

We need men like you in business and banking. Men who don't simply want to accumulate wealth and help others to do so, but who see how harnessing the positive potential of money* can bring liberation and so much good. Men who are determined to bring equality and justice to the boardrooms and the lowest rungs of any business; who will insert ethics into organizations that make a profit from other people's personal loss.

*Money isn't evil remember, but the love of it is the root of all kinds of awfulness. If this is your route, be very, very careful. Start your career by being painfully and sacrificially generous, otherwise you'll probably never develop the habit later on.

The world needs men like you in the media and entertainment, helping to shape the messages and the stories that current and emerging generations will hear. Men who bring good news into an industry that's often obsessed with bad. Men who report the news fairly and with integrity, and vow to clear up the messes of previous generations who hacked phones and put pictures of naked women on the news pages.

Men like you are vital in the world of emerging technology. If that's your path, then you will play a part in shaping the world. We need men in the big tech companies who know the value but also the limitations of the online world, and of our relentless obsession with progress and advancement. We need men who will have the character to say no, when someone is about to make a decision that will land the world in a post-apocalyptic sci-fi movie.*

*You could be the guy that stops Skynet (see The Terminator if you haven't already).

We need good men who will invest in education at every level, shaping and influencing kids, young people and students to become the people that they were made to be too. We need good men in healthcare, who can't be bought by a pharmaceutical company with a high-class golf day. We need men of integrity and honour in our armed forces, and in our emergency services.

If you're so inclined, we badly need men who understand themselves, and who have committed to this journey of developing their character, in the Church. Men who are not interested in their own profile and fame, or in the powerful feeling they get from leading others, but who are genuine pastors, building hope in those who lack it, and empowering those who years of flawed church history have left trailing behind.

And the list goes on and on. If you've understood who you are, why you're here, and what kind of life you're going to live, then the world needs you badly, in farming, in architecture, in nursing, in retail, in fashion, in sport, and in every industry, career or pursuit you can think of. And in the other stuff you do with your life – whether you're a poet or a mountaineer – the world needs you to consistently be the man you were made to be.

Your life is an adventure, and it's not designed to be lived alone. God made you for community with your friends, family and perhaps also someone really special. More even than that though, he made you for friendship with himself, through Jesus.

He wants to be part of the highs and the lows. From my experience, he wants to give you a hand up at some moments, and console you in the times when it doesn't quite go to plan. He wants to be a part of continuously shaping you, day after day, as if his design and creation of you isn't quite finished yet.

He wants to join you on the adventure, like Samwise Gamgee in *The Lord of the Rings*, or Donkey in *Shrek*.* He wants to be your companion, your friend and your guide. Why wouldn't we want that? They say that if your dreams don't scare you, they're not big enough, so why on earth would we want to run headlong towards them without support?

I hope I don't go to hell for that comparison.

The final part of understanding who you're made to be, even beyond the moment when you realize what you're here to do, is the slow realization that you don't need to do it on your own.

A man who truly gets this, invests some of his resources in his relationship with that companion. The more we know God, the more we benefit from knowing him, and so as old-fashioned as it might sound, there's huge value in reading about him and talking with him.

The Bible is old. It's hard to read in places. Yet it is unquestionably the wisest and most helpful book ever written. You will find a thousand times more wisdom in it about what it means to grow into your fullest potential than I could ever hope to offer on these pages. That's because, in a way that I can't begin to explain here,* it's kind of *alive*. Or at least, the Holy Spirit – God on earth among us – brings it to life and interprets it to us. That's why you can be reading a passage written two thousand years ago and know with strange certainty that it makes sense of your current feelings about that relationship that just broke down, or the job you just got.

This isn't because I don't have any idea, but because it would take a long time, and we're drawing things to a close here. Suffice to say: when we read the Bible, the Holy Spirit helps us to understand it in a way that feels fresh and relevant to our lives today.

Finding some time to read the Bible each day is a great investment of your time, and a sure-fire way to build your personal wisdom. Even if you don't feel ready for that, I hope I've done enough in this book to convince you to check out more of the stories of Jesus. There's no better way to learn from him as a role model than to read his words and the stories written about him in Matthew, Mark, Luke and John.

Most fundamentally of all though, our relationship with God thrives through daily communication. Prayer is just the act of you talking into the air, and believing that someone can hear you. Although that seems crazy – and some have speculated that it is indeed the first sign of madness – the story of my life, and of literally billions of others, is that somehow, perhaps implausibly, someone does hear us.

What's more, in the act of speaking to God, some other strange stuff seems to happen. In my experience, he's involved in our thoughts even as we pray; we find ourselves – even as we're praying – being steered towards a certain answer, or course of action. In moments of silence, some people report that they actually hear the voice of God, whispering back at them. And then even if neither of those things happens – and for many people they don't – he often seems to respond through action; through what is either divine intervention or a mad series of coincidences, depending on how you want to look at it.

The best way to involve God in the long-term pursuit of our purpose and adventure is simply to speak to him, regularly. And the great thing is: even in the act of focusing on him and praying into these things, we're reminded over and again of the decisions we've made about our character and purpose.

This relationship, above all else, is what you were made for. If you embrace that, everything else inevitably clicks into place. My own journey to Hollywood and back wasn't marked with human success, but it doesn't really matter. What counts is that I got to do it all with the God who made me, and in the process I learned exactly who I was made to be. Not a screenwriter – successful or otherwise – but a beloved child of the Creator of the universe, living out his purpose on earth, with an ear to heaven.

Think about . . .

As you reach the end of this book, what have been some of the major things you've realized about yourself, and the person you want to become?

Think about that phrase: 'life to the full'. What does life in all its fullness look like for you?

What do you think your purpose is? How might that translate into the decisions you make about future education, employment or career?

How can you involve God in the everyday journey of discovering and pursuing your purpose?

Read this bit last

Men don't read books. That's another classic bit of gender pigeon-holing, right there. Well guess what? Unless you're standing in a shop, and have somehow thought that the best place to start when checking out this book would be the final page, you have just disproved another lazy stereotype.

How many others could you now disprove, if you seek to put just a few of these ideas into practice? Could you be a man who knows who he is, and what he stands for? Could you be a guy who resists classic temptations, and sidesteps easy pitfalls? Could you be a man who knows how to cry, and how to build real friendships with members of both sexes?

Could you somehow be a guy who masters self-control, and isn't ruled by his primal instincts? Could you bring the different complex areas of your life into balance, from how much time you spend glued to your phone, even through to how much of your life you spend in prayer and contemplation? Might you be a man who can hold down a relationship that isn't based on sex, or even one who waits until the right relationship to ever have sex in the first place? Might you become someone who claims to stand for some things, and then actually lives up to that claim?

All of that is my prayer for you as I write the final sentences of this book. I pray that you are enabled to resume your own life-long journey towards truly knowing your place and purpose in this world. I pray that you discover, more and more, the incredible, future-changing man you were created to be, and step into your destiny with reckless abandon. And most of all, I pray that you will be able to draw your identity as a man not from past experiences, genetics or decisions you've made, but from the unswerving knowledge that you were handmade by a God who says to you, day after day, and minute after minute of your life:

I love you, man.

Thanks

I want to thank a few people for their investment in this project, and in me. Tony Collins at SPCK – thanks for believing in me, and never asking me to sell out in order to sell a few books. Thanks to James Chapman, Rachel Gardner, Jess Gibson, Joe Hartropp, Charles Merritt, Lucie Shuker and Rachel Warwick for reading chapters, offering feedback and generally being incredibly encouraging when I was struggling to write another word. Thanks to Joel, who gave up his precious evenings to read through the entire book, and informed me it was 'surprisingly funny for you, Dad'. Thanks to Jo for all the cups of coffee, all the 'keep going's, and for occasionally telling me to stop and get some sleep. Most of all though, thanks to the utterly sensational young people of St Mary's, Reigate, on whom I may possibly have road-tested about 90 per cent of this material without their knowledge. I edited out some absolute garbage because of you.

Also by Martin Saunders

500 Prayers for Young People

The Beautiful Disciplines

Chased by the Dragon, Caught by the Lamb (with Brian Morris)

Convicted or Condemned? (with Dez Brown)

David Street's Christmas Diary

East End to East Coast

England's Messiah

Games with a Purpose (with Jimmy Young)

The Ideas Factory

The Power and the Glory (with Arthur White)

The Think Tank

Youth Work from Scratch